How to Customize Your Star

Doug Mitchel

Published by:
Wolfgang Publications Inc.
Stillwater, MN 55082
www.wolfpub.com

Legals

First published in 2009 by Wolfgang Publications Inc.,
PO Box 223, Stillwater MN 55082

ISBN-13: 978-1-929133-65-9
ISBN-10: 1-929133-65-0

Printed and bound in China.

How to Customize Your Star

Foreword

Fifteen years ago, there were two rules when it came to customizing: No. 1, leave customizing to professionals and No. 2, only customize a Harley-Davidson®. Boy, things have changed a lot in those 15 years. Since Jesse James appeared on the Discovery Channel, customizing has never been the same! Soon, motorcycles became more and more popular and demand exceeded supply regarding available units and those customizing. Yamaha heard the call and answered back with the Royal Star then followed that with the V-Star 1100 then the Road Star, V-Star 650 and the STAR line was born.

I'm proud to say that I was one of the few who led the charge and customized several Royal Stars that broke from the pack and stood front and center at the nation's most prominent shows begging to be looked at, and people did. After that, it was all I could do to keep up with the demand for products. In the early days of customizing Metric motorcycles, it was all about buying products for Harley-Davidsons® then taking them apart and refabricating them to suit a builder's needs.

As sales of Metric motorcycles increased (especially STAR motorcycles), so did the demand for the products. Baron Custom Accessories was right there answering the call, but others responded as well. This brought more options for custom covers, exhausts, Big Air Kits (BAK), handlebars and ultimately what drove me to release copies of the award winning fenders, side covers, and tank extensions I'd created for our show bikes and many bikes shown by Yamaha Motor Corporation.

It was the release of these body parts coupled with Baron's unique handlebars and bolt-on accessories that ultimately drove, inspired and motivated many owners to build their own custom bikes. Though I've designed more than a thousand products, the one thing I never thought to do was to sit down and write a book telling virtually anyone with enough skill to twist a throttle and keep a bike on two wheels, how to create and build a custom bike of their own. Thankfully, Doug Mitchel used his writing craft and Kody Wisner his mechanical skills and the duo created this Metric masterpiece. Together, they created a step-by-step tool that will allow anyone with a little initiative, elbow grease and a lot less money than hiring someone to do it, to create and build a bike of their own.

I encourage you to read on, be inspired and create an attention-getter that gives you rock star status! Even though the book may expel many of the secrets that have kept bike builders like us employed, the good news is that is gives us time to put rubber to the pavement.

Ride a nice day…

John "Baron" Vaughan-Chaldy

Acknowledgements

First and foremost I have to extend thanks to John and Jill Parham for their continued assistance in so many of my motorcycle related projects. I have worked with John for more than twenty years, and watched his business grow into the powerhouse that it is today. If not for his efforts we'd have no bike to work on, or a place to create this custom Yamaha. My only hope is that some of his well-deserved success wears off on me.

- To Kody "Wis-Kid" Wisner, for his expert handling of all things mechanical. He was a part of the first meetings regarding this project and turned every wrench to make it real. His skills at all things motorcycle became obvious in the first hour of our working together, and grew more evident with every passing journey to J&P.

- Shannon "The Sky is Falling" Appleby, for his hands-on assistance when it was required and for filming the entire procedure to morph the Yamaha from factory to custom. As long as my footage doesn't end up on an episode of COPS, I'll be grateful for his help.

- Nicole Ridge, whose skills at marketing helped to bring this deal to the J&P table an get the ball rolling, and for providing a coherent "go-to" contact during the sorting of details, all of which needed to be addressed before the green light was turned on.

- Andrea LaRonde for stepping in and photographing the images needed to complete this journey (pages 127-129). Her efforts illustrate that she has mad skills in the photographic world, and provided the pictures that saved me a fifth trip to Anamosa.

Doug Mitchel

Introduction

Since the dawn of the motorcycle we have seen proof that most riders are not content with the factory offerings. No sooner had the first machines been ridden home than people began altering their new craft to suit their needs and style.

After World War II ended, returning soldiers were anxious to enjoy their freedom, and many threw their boots over surplus motorcycles that they picked up at bargain rates. Being primarily military issue machines made them ripe for civilian tweaks, and the race was on. The first "chopper" was built by removing heavy steel fenders, and excess parts were chopped off or altered to provide a sleeker appearance for the street.

The custom craze kicked into high gear during the late 1950s and into the '60s. Not only did the craze grow in strength, but we also began to see some new faces in the motorcycle market. Honda, Kawasaki, Suzuki and Yamaha all brought their style of machine to these shores in the early part of the '60s. While many scoffed at the tint, two-stroke offerings, others flocked to the showrooms to get their hands on one. Their smaller size and ease of operation appealed to a large number of buyers, and that number was growing faster than the industry could keep up with.

Yamaha sold their first motorcycles in the States in the latter part of 1960, and the brand was on par with other Japanese built machines. As the market matured, riders begged for more power and bigger models. As variety ran rampant we began to see specific ranges of cycles being formed. The original standard issue designs were joined by sport and touring machines. Although they did their appointed tasks well, some riders desired something that looked more like a traditional American made machine, but included the latest in Japanese technology. The resulting models were penned "cruisers," and the name skyrocketed in popularity. The middle '80s saw the first bikes falling into the new category - and their range and success continues today.

The 1996 Royal Star was the first in Yamaha's new Star family and it embodied the best that the cruiser field had to offer. A 1294cc V-4 motor looked the part of a Milwaukee mill while providing more power and smoothness. The almost immediate success of the new Star brand fostered a wide range of models in the years that followed. Some carried smaller motors in their frames for novice riders, while others went to the extreme end of the spectrum. The 2009 models range from a 250cc Star - all the way up to four different models powered by 113 cubic inch power plants. Not only has the model line grown, but the available options and accessories boggle the mind. Not only does Yamaha offer its own line of custom bits, but aftermarket makers have also jumped on the bandwagon.

The changes made to our 2008 Midnight Star were chosen to show you just some of the things that can be achieved. The myriad of options on the market today ensure that any efforts taken by individual owners will result in a truly unique ride. J&P offers a huge array of parts for your Star as well as the technical expertise to get you the right parts when you aren't sure of what might fit.

Chapter One

Saddles and Floorboards

Make it Fit You Like a Glove

One of the best parts about buying a Road Star is the wide array of options and accessories you can add to make the machine your own. While many may enhance performance or appearance, the comfort of the rider and passenger are paramount to the enjoyment of your new bike.

The stock saddle and floorboards work well for most people, but a long day on the road can quickly bring certain aspects of your comfort to bear. Obviously everyone has their own body with no two being alike, so there are no right or wrong answers here. Alterations to the seat and footrests

The factory saddle is a two-piece affair and provides adequate comfort for most people.

won't affect your warranty either, making them a safe bet if you plan on keeping your ride for a long period of time.

In this chapter we will explore several variations in the seating department and upgrade the floorboards for a more custom appearance. The changes you'll see here are fairly easy, but will radically alter the way your Yamaha feels after many hours of touring. Before making a decision, ask around and see what friends have to say about the seats they bought. Their opinion may not match your needs, but at least you can learn a bit more about the options in the market. J&P stocks a large selection of saddles and will be a great place to do your one stop shopping.

With Kody seated on the stock seat with factory bars, we see the relation between his hands and boots and can compare this to the seat options soon to be seen.

Our first seat option comes from Saddlemen (J&P Part # ZZ80087), and is called the Saddlehyde. Beneath the upholstered surface is a gel that adds comfort while bringing a new level of style to the game.

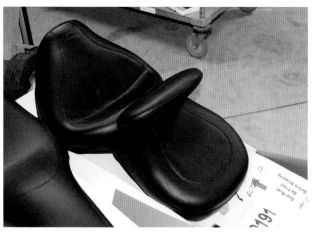

A second choice will be from Mustang (J&P Part # ZZ80136), and is a more traditional saddle that includes a backrest for added rider comfort.

With the main section set aside, slide the passenger pillion forward to remove it from the Road Star.

Using a 10mm Allen wrench, loosen and remove the fastener that holds the passenger seat in place.

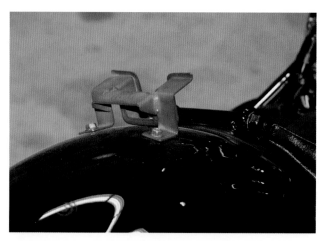

The factory mounting bracket will also need to be removed prior to installing the Saddlemen seat.

Turning the ignition key allows you to lift the front portion of the Yamaha seat free of its mounts.

The front hoop bracket on the Yamaha seat will need to be transferred to the Saddlemen seat, use the same mounting bolts to attach to the new saddle.

This is the bracket that needs to be removed from the Yamaha seat first.

Remove the three bolts that hold the factory rear seat mount in place. Neither the bracket, nor the bolts will be needed for the Saddlemen pillion installation.

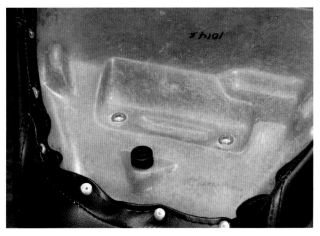

The Saddlemen seat is pre-drilled to accept the Yamaha bracket.

The Saddlemen seat attaches to the Yamaha mounting clasp in the front.

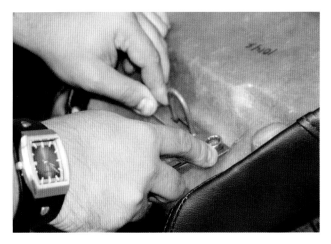

Once pulled off the Yamaha seat, the bracket can be bolted in place on the Saddlemen seat.

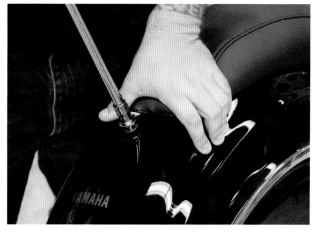

With the front clipped into place, a 10mm bolt secures the rear portion of the new saddle.

Kody shows us how the Saddlemen seat positions him on the bike. The design of the saddle allows the rider to move around a bit and that comes in handy when spending hours on the open road.

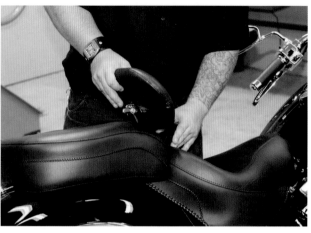

The rider's backrest slips easily into place and can also be removed within a moment's notice.

After removing the Saddlemen seat, we are ready to install our next option. The Mustang seat comes with mounting bracket attached and can simply be latched into place using the Yamaha mechanism.

The Mustang seat is much different than the Saddlemen model. We can see how it affects the position of Kody's feet and hands.

The same 10mm fastener holds the rear portion of the Mustang seat in place.

The Yamaha passenger footpegs give you a place to hang your boots, but offer little in the way of style.

To remove the Yamaha pegs, use pliers to straighten the cotter pin, then pull it out of the retainer pin. Slide the retainer pin free and remove the peg.

The rider's floorboards will now get a matching set of covers to dress them up a bit.

We install a set of Kuryakyn ISO Wing Footrests (530-170 and adapter ZZ53090) to add style and comfort. Simply place the footrest in the factory mount and use the retainer pin to hold in place.

Always read the manufacturer's instructions prior to installing any new component.

Jessica now has a more comfortable place to put her boots when she and Kody take to the streets.

Fold the floorboard up to gain access to the 8mm fastener that needs to be removed. Once removed, the factory rubber pad can be pulled off of the base.

11

The new floorboards will bolt directly to the Yamaha mounting holes.

Tighten the new fastener to secure the Kuryakyn floorboard in place.

Place the Kuryakyn floorboard into the mounting holes and push into position.

The next step in the dress-up parade will be a new Kuryakyn brake pedal pad (J&P Part # ZZ27270). Simply pry the Yamaha pad loose and remove it from the pedal.

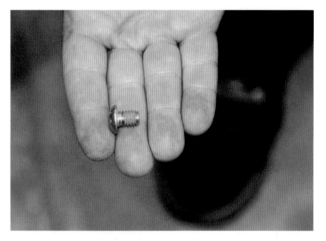

The supplied hardware comes complete with thread locking compound, which will keep the new fastener in place.

Use an Allen wrench to remove the four screws on the bottom of the new cover.

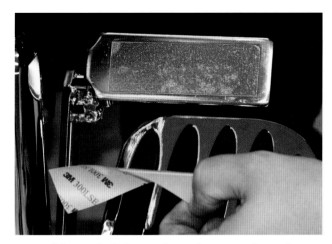

Use rubbing alcohol, or other solvent, to clean the surface of the pedal before adhering the double-sided tape to the face. Hold the lower mounting plate in position and line up the top section. Once held in place by the tape, replace the four screws to complete the job.

The new Kuryakyn footboards and brake pedal cover add a nice touch and a bit of flash to your Star.

Chapter One Part Number and Supplier

Page	Description	J&P Part #	Supplier name and part #
Pg. 7	Saddlemen Saddlehyde seat	ZZ80087	Drag Specialties Y3385FJ
Pg. 8	Vintage 2 piece seat w/ backrest	ZZ80136	Mustang 79191
Pg. 11	Kuryakyn ISO wing boards	530-170	Kuryakyn 4452
	Footpeg adapters	ZZ53090	Kuryakyn 8811
Pg. 12	Kuryakyn brake pedal cover	ZZ27270	Kuryakyn 8858

Chapter Two

The Bar Scene

Change Handlebars to Better Suit Your Needs

One of the easiest ways to alter the appearance and stance of your Road Star is by changing the handlebars. By installing a different set of bars you can revise the way you fit on the saddle by moving your hand location. Changing the bars

may also do little more than give your Star a look that's different than your neighbor's, and that may be enough reason.

By choosing a Road Star, you rode home on a machine that has a wide number of bar options

Kody is seated on the Road Star in its stock trim and you can see his relation to the bars and floorboards. He stands 5'- 4" so keep that in mind when comparing the images to your own stature. It is suggested that the seat and fuel tank be removed prior to the removal of the factory bars to avoid scratching the paint or chrome.

on the menu. You can easily go wider, lower or way tall, like the ones we've selected for this build. While "ape hangers" aren't for everyone, they do provide a distinctive appearance to an otherwise factory ride. Of course changing from factory bars to another set may require that the cables and wires that provide control are shortened or lengthened depending on which set you select. The super tall bars we are installing require the wiring loom to be extended and a fresh set of control cables to be mounted to ensure proper operation of the clutch, throttle and electrical switches.

Use a fine edged tool to remove the decorative caps that cover the mounting bolts that lie beneath.

Before you even purchase a new set of bars, try to get some exposure to how each different set will affect your riding position and access to the brake pedal and shift lever. Those of us who lack in stature need to take extra care that the bars we choose don't pull our feet away from the controls. We have provided a few illustrations of how different bars will alter the placement of the rider's hands, but a personal choice should be made with hands-on experience. By changing the width and height of the bars, you will find yourself being forced into a new stance, and your comfort and safety still trump a cool new look.

With all four caps removed you can now see the exposed Allen head fasteners that hold the handlebar clamp in place.

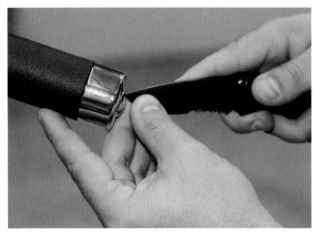

More decorative caps conceal the bar-end fasteners that need to be accessed. Remove each one carefully to avoid scratching the surface.

Remove the bottom screw from the throttle switch housing and loosen the two Allen screws from the face of the assembly.

An allen wrench is now used to loosen and remove the bolt that holds the bar end weights in place.

Use a small screwdriver to remove the cable retainer clip.

Once loosened, the bar end weights can be pulled from each end of the factory bars. Be sure to retain all of your factory hardware in case you later decide to return your bike to stock trim.

Loosen the collars that hold the mirrors in position, then spin the mirrors free of their mounting holes.

Slip the throttle control housing free of the handlebar, taking care not to unplug the connectors in the process.

With all the control hardware removed you can turn to loosening and removing the four screws that hold the upper bar mount in place.

Remove the screws holding the clutch control housing and pull it free of the bars.

Now that all four screws are loose, the entire assembly can be lifted from its position. DO NOT let the bars fall and damage the tank or the controls.

Since the left hand grip is attached directly to the bars it will take some convincing to remove.

By mounting a set of Baron's Star Bars (J&P Part # ZZ50331) we can quickly see the difference in Kody's riding posture.

17

The next set of test bars are also from Baron's. The Big Johnson bars (J&P Part #ZZ50020) feature a larger diameter tube that enhances style. You can also see the altered posture gained by the use of these bars.

The next stop in our bar hopping adventure will be the Baron's Hot Rod Drag bars (J&P Part # ZZ-50332) with integral risers. The supplied bolts must be slipped up through the Yamaha mounting holes.

Our next bars require the removal of the Yamaha risers. Simply remove the two mounting nuts beneath the triple tree.

Line up the mounting bolts to the threaded holes in the bars and tighten by hand before taking a wrench to them.

With the two nuts removed, you can lift the Yamaha risers off their mounting location.

Once properly located, tighten to factory specs.

The Hot Rod Drag bars place the grips in Kody's hands in a fairly natural position, but of course he has chosen a more radical approach for this build.

Kody has selected a pair of Baron's Kong bars (J&P Part # ZZ50021) for the build. WARNING! Some states have limits on the height of the bars, so be sure to check your rule book before getting too high.

Now we can gain access to the wiring that will be lengthened with this set of Ape Hangers. With any job like this, take care to ensure adequate free play when turning the bars from side to side.

After unplugging the headlight and setting it aside, you'll see a rat's nest of wiring inside. Color coding is used to separate each wire and its use, and we'll visit that department when you extend the harness.

Longer throttle cables will also need to be used, so loosen the nuts holding the Yamaha cables in place.

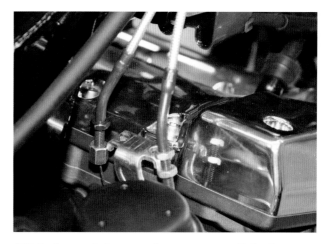

With the retaining nuts loose, you can slide the cables free of their mount at the carburetor.

Remove the two screws that hold the sections of the throttle control housing together so you can access the ends of the cables inside.

To remove the factory brake line from the master cylinder, loosen the banjo bolt that holds it in place. Keep a cloth handy to catch any falling brake fluid.

With the throttle housing now open you can easily remove the cable ends from their locations and pull the cables free of the assembly.

Slide the brake control housing onto the new bars and snug up the fasteners, but DO NOT tighten yet.

Locate the connector inside the headlight bucket and disconnect the loom from the internal wiring. A Baron's Kong Bar Cable Kit (J&P Part #383-865) required when adding the much taller bars to your Star.

Next, slide the throttle control housing onto the bar and tighten the screws. Replace clutch control housing on the left bar end, snug fasteners. Also the electronic switch controls to determine the new length of cable.

Remove the banjo bolt from the brake line at the junction box mounted behind the turn signal light bar.

When reinstalling the brake line, be sure to use the factory banjo bolt and copper washers in the same fashion they were removed.

Connect the new extended brake line to the master cylinder using the Yamaha banjo bolt and copper washers.

Reattach the new brake line to the junction box. The brakes will need to be bled before riding the bike, so if no other modifications are being made to the brake system do that now.

The clutch cable will now need to be removed from the shift lever on the left side of the motor.

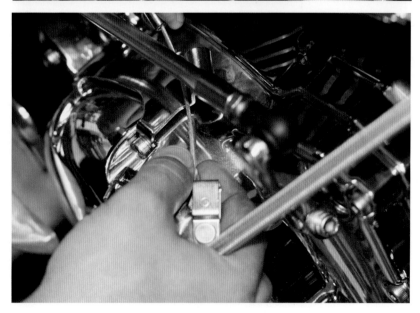

Install the new longer cable at both ends. Final adjustment can be made, once the reassembly is complete, for proper free play in the cable per Yamaha specifications.

Apply grip glue to the new bar end and slide the new left hand grip into place. This needs to be done quickly as the glue sets up fairly fast.

Reinsert the idle cable back into the throttle housing first, followed by the throttle cable second. Do not tighten the mounting nuts yet.

Reinstall both cables into the carburetor next, being sure to connect them in their proper slots before tightening. Test throttle action for smooth play when bars are turned in both directions to ensure nothing is pinched before tightening all required nuts.

Baron suggests you add twenty inches of wire to the existing loom for adequate clearance. Once this number is confirmed, begin cutting the black rubber sleeve from the wiring harness. Be careful not to cut the wires inside or nick their insulation.

With the protective sleeve trimmed back you can see the wires, and color coded system, that will allow you to join it with the extension loom.

For a neater appearance upon completion, we will be using a set of West Eagle risers (J&P Part # ZZ50981). This will allow more clearance for the wiring since we will be passing it through the bars.

Now that the sleeve has been removed from a section of the wiring you can begin the splicing process.

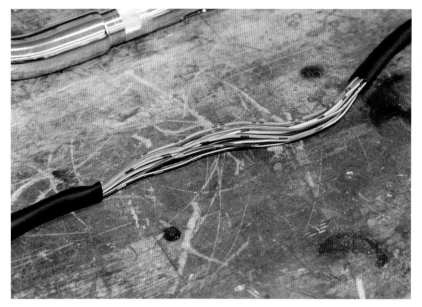

A generic Wire Harness Extension (J&P Part #383-294) will be used to lengthen the Yamaha wires for use. Be sure to create a written list of which Yamaha wire is being spliced to which generic wire. This will be needed after the extension has been passed through the bars and reconnection to the factory plugs is made.

Stagger the cut in each wire by 1 inch so that all of the splices won't end up in the same position and cause an excess thickness. Since we'll be passing the loom through the handlebars we need to keep the completed harness thin.

You only need to strip about a half an inch from the end of each section of wire for adequate splicing.

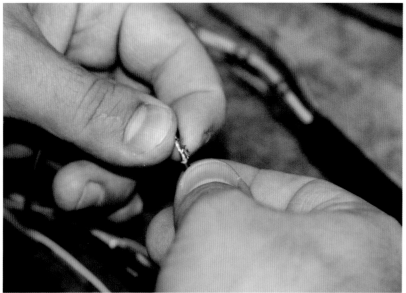

Once the extension wire has been cut to the proper length, splice it with an existing wire using a Western Union style splice.

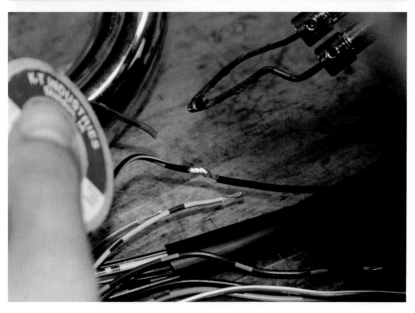

After the wire is spliced it needs to be soldered for a proper connection.

Once the solder has cooled and you are certain of a complete splice, cover the splice with heat shrink and apply heat to reduce for a complete seal. Caution needs to be taken to ensure a complete connection at each joint. Once the loom has been fed through the handlebars no one wants to think about pulling it all apart to find a spot that has broken.

When all of the splices are complete, wrap the entire length of the harness with tape, or heat shrink, prior to inserting into the bars. Slowly feed the completed harness through the opening beneath the control housing.

The wrapped harness will eventually reach the lower opening of the bars and be ready for reinstallation. The process of passing the wires through the bars is more easily achieved with the bars off of the bike, and the time saved will be worth the headache of removal.

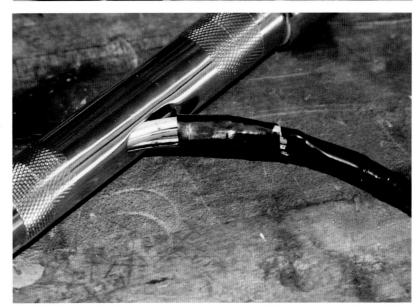

Using your color chart from before, connect the ends of the extension harness to the Yamaha wiring that was severed in bottom photo on page 25.

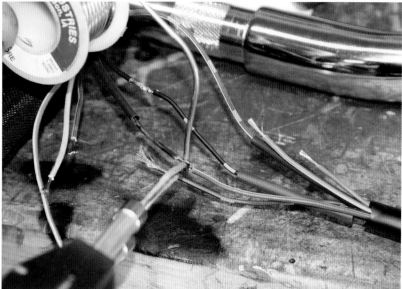

Once again you need to splice all the wires using a Western Union style twist.

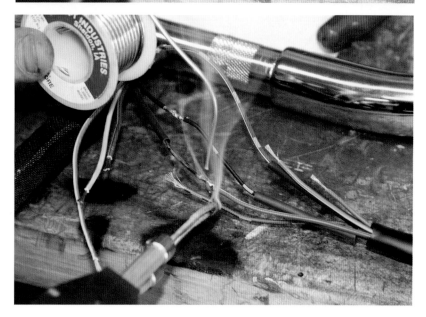

Each splice will also need to be soldered for a complete connection.

Heat shrink over each soldered splice is the next step to ensure a solid and safe connection.

After each splice has been completed, the entire length of wires can be wrapped in heat shrink, or electrical tape, for a cleaner look and safer transition.

The space between the two West Eagle Risers will allow plenty of space for the wire bundles to pass through and be reconnected.

Kody now places the first of the two bullet caps in place to secure the handlebar's attachment.

The second bullet cap is now installed and the Allen head screws are tightened to secure the bar in place. Before tightening completely, it is suggested that you sit on the bike and confirm the position of the bars before turning the last screw into place.

With the handlebars now secure, you can pass the wiring harness through the triple tree and into the back of the headlight bucket.

Pull the harness through the opening until there is enough clearance for installation.

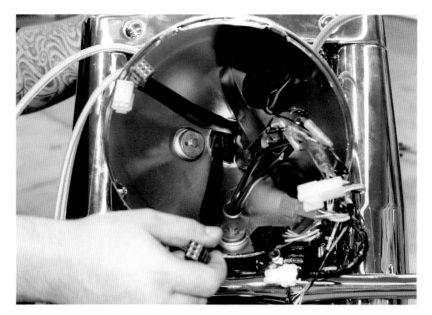

If you have chosen to remove the bars to install the wiring harness, you now need to reattach the clutch cable and adjust for free play.

Reconnect the color coded plugs that will be hidden by the headlight.

Reattach the throttle assembly if it was removed prior to the harness installation.
Inset: The master cylinder will also need to be reattached if it was removed to ease the wiring assembly.

Be sure to plug in the brake light plug before proceeding.

The banjo bolt and washers can now be reattached as well. The brakes can be bled unless further work will be done to the system.

Reinstall the headlight and insert the two screws that hold it in place.

With the hardware back in place, and the wiring harness extended, we can see the full effect of the Kong bars on the Road Star.

Chapter Two Part Number and Supplier

Page	Description	J&P Part #	Supplier name and part #
Pg. 17	Baron's Star bar	ZZ50331	Barons BA-7300-00
Pg. 18	Baron's Big Johnson bar	ZZ50020	Barons BA-7300-02
Pg. 18	Baron's Hot Rod Drag bars	ZZ50332	Baron's BA-7301-00
Pg. 19	Baron's Kong bars	ZZ50021	Baron's BA-7300-06
Pg. 24	Bullet risers	ZZ50981	West Eagle 0472
Pg. 20	Baron's Kong Bar Cable kit	383-865	Baron's BA-8022KT-KB
Pg. 25	Handlebar wiring extension	383-294	Designs by Novello NIL-WH20CC

Chapter Three

Lowering the Suspension

Drop it in the Weeds

The Road Star is not the biggest motorcycle on the market, but some riders may find it to be top heavy and cumbersome at low speeds. Riders with shorter legs may also have difficulty while parking or moving their Star around the garage.

The best way to correct this issue is by altering the suspension, thus lowering the center of gravity. Altered suspension will also drop the seat height, allowing the rider's feet to more easily reach the ground. There are a few different ways to modify

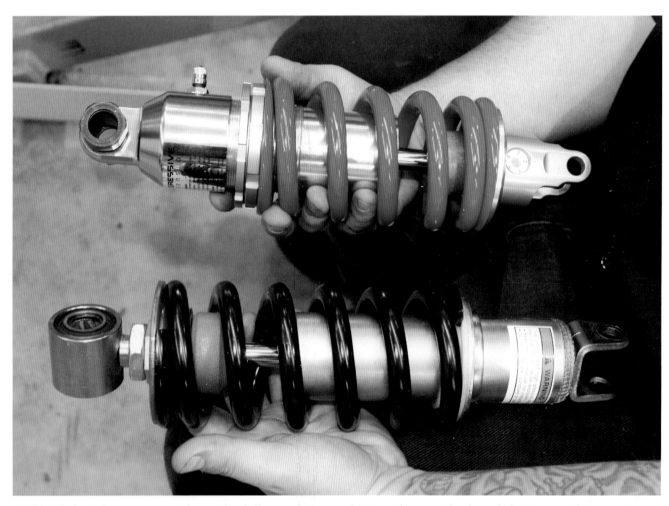

Held side by side, you can easily see the difference between the Yamaha rear shock and the improved Progressive unit we'll be installing. The adjustable Progressive shock will enhance the ride of your Star. Place it lower to the ground, and provide some adjustability.

your Star's suspension, but we'll use kits that are already engineered for peak performance. While dropping the back end of the machine, our upgraded shock will also deliver an enhanced ride, especially when two-up. The new components will provide additional adjustment, giving the rider a way to customize how his or her Star rolls down the road. The Progressive 420 Series model we have chosen drops the back end an inch. To save some green, you can purchase a different spring

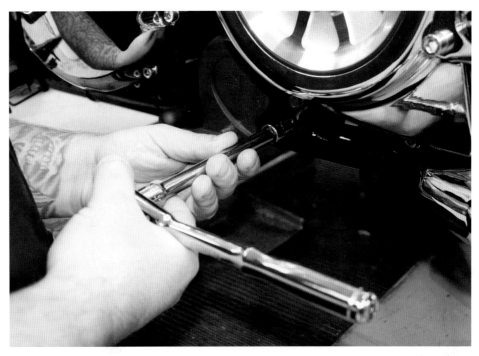

To gain access to the shock mounting bolts you first need to remove the two bolts holding the horn, in place. Remove the bolts, unplug the horn and set it aside for reinstallation later.

for the rear shock, but some additional steps and tools will be required to swap out the coils. Making this change will raise the spring rate from 760 to 980 pounds, and lower the bike 1.5 inches. For those who are happy with the performance of their factory shock, but would still like to lower their bike, a lowering link (J&P Part # ZZ70407) from Baron will do the job.

When choosing to lower any motorcycle's suspension, be sure you'll have adequate clearance for chassis bits and exhaust. There's no sense in dropping a bike's ride height only to find it drags on the pavement, or bottoms out at the first sign of irregularity in the road.

Once these steps are complete we'll have a Road Star that can more easily be managed by a shorter rider, or simply make the machine roll on a lower stance giving it a more aggressive appearance.

Loosen, but DO NOT remove the front mounting bolt of the shock.

Use a floor jack to raise the chassis slightly, taking weight off of the rear wheel. You only need to provide a small amount of clearance between the tire and the floor.

Once removed, set the mounting bolt and nut aside for reuse later.

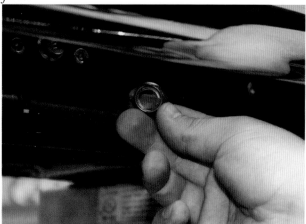

From the right side of the chassis, remove the nut from the front mount of the shock.

With the bolt removed, you can lower the shock mount free. You can now see the bushings and "dog bones" that allow the shock to do its job when mounted in place.

From the left side of the chassis, pull the long mounting bolt free. You may need to tap it loose from the other side of the chassis to remove it more easily.

Since we have added some chrome accessories to the Star, an Allen wrench is needed to remove the screws holding it in place and allow access to the rear axle.

With the 2 screws removed you can take the chrome trim piece off the rear axle mount.

Prior to removing the rear axle you'll need to loosen the threaded section from the left side of the chassis.

The second section of chrome trim will now be removed from the right side of the axle giving us access to the axle nut.

Once the threads are loose the entire axle can be removed from the chassis.

Loosen and remove the axle nut and set aside for reinstallation.

Loosen, but DO NOT remove the bolt that holds the rear brake bracket in place.

Move the rear tire forward slightly and slip the drive belt off the pulley.

Remove the four fasteners that hold the lower section of the inner fender in place, then pull the piece free. All of this will be reused, so keep the proper bolts with the correct component.

The rear tire and wheel can now be removed for access to the rest of the shock mounts.

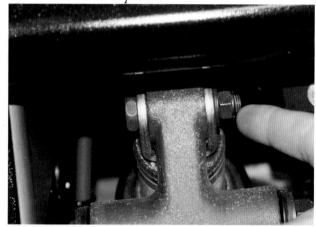

The rear shock mount is now exposed, and Kody is pointing to the upper bolt and nut that need to be removed. You need a 14mm and 17mm wrench for removal.

Remove the three bolts that secure the plastic belt guard in place, then pull the assembly free of the chassis.

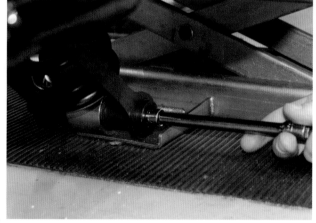

The front half of the shock is held to the "dog bones" with a hollow shaft that needs to be pushed as shown. We used an extension with a socket of the correct size for this job.

With both ends of the shock now free, you can lower the Yamaha shock out of its position.

Align the hollow shaft, the opening in the "dog bones", and the lower mounting hole of the Progressive shock, and tap the shaft through the assembly.

Slide the Progressive 420 Series shock (J&P Part # ZZ70485) into place and slip the factory bolt back through the upper mounting hole of the Yamaha bracket.

Reinsert the long shock bolt through left side of the shaft. Once through the lower shock assembly, attach the nut and tighten to spec. The lower section of the inner fender can now be reattached.

Reinstall the upper washer and nut, and tighten to factory specifications.

Reconnect the wires to the horn, and reinstall with the two factory bolts.

We are adding a chrome belt guard from Baron's (J&P Part # ZZ60073) in place of the black factory unit. The Baron part bolts to the same location as the Yamaha piece.

Lift the back wheel back into place.

Slip the drive belt back onto the pulley before sliding the axle bolt back into place.

Slide the axle through the wheel, making sure to align the adjusting plate before tightening the axle in place.

Install the axle bolt and tighten to factory specs.

To begin lowering the front forks, remove the two bolts that hold each of the brake calipers in position. To keep them out of your way you may want to zip tie them to the frame.

Place the jack under the front frame tubes and raise to extend the front forks, unloading the tension.

Loosen the fork tube caps on the top of each fork leg.

Use an Allen wrench to loosen the axle and pinch bolts at the bottom of the fork leg.

Loosen and remove the front axle from the fork legs.

With the axle removed, you can take the front tire off of the bike and set it aside.

Loosen and remove the steering stem nut found at the top of the triple tree.

Loosen the upper triple tree pinch bolts on both sides of the fork.

Carefully lift the upper triple tree from the fork assembly.

Carefully remove each of the upper fork leg covers and set them aside.

The contents of the Baron's front end lowering kit (J&P Part # ZZ23160) can be seen here. The clear sections of PVC tube will need to be cut to length prior to insertion.

Remove the large flat spacers, then loosen the pair of pinch bolts at the top of each fork leg. Once removed, you can slide each fork leg free.

Loosen the damper rod screw at the bottom of the fork leg. WARNING! When this screw is loose you should prepare for a flow of fork oil with a catch tray and cloth.

Slowly loosen and remove the upper fork tube cap. WARNING! The spring that lies beneath the cap is under high pressure, so use caution once the cap is free to avoid having the spring damage anything in its path.

With the cap removed the spring is now exposed and can be lifted out of the fork tube.

Set the Yamaha spring aside and slowly pour the fork oil into a receptacle. It will NOT be reused and must be disposed of properly.

With the fork oil drained from the tube, you can now remove the lower damper rod screw completely. Use caution not to lose the brass washer used to seal the screw.

After removing the top out spring, slide the Baron's top out spacer onto the damper tube and replace the spring as shown. Slide the damper assembly back into the fork leg and line up the threads before reinserting the damper screw and brass washer. Clean excess fork oil off the screw before using to ensure a positive seal when tightened.

Right: Insert the Baron's spring into the fork tube and set the assembly aside.

The PVC preload spacers will need to be cut to a length of 6.3 inches before being installed. Be sure to cut the material with a square end to ensure positive positioning when installed.

Measure 18.7 ounces (Yamaha specs) of NEW 5W fork oil. Be sure to check the manual for your bike to ensure that this is the proper quantity for your motorcycle.

Right: Pour the fork oil into the top of the fork leg SLOWLY and tap the assembly lightly on the work surface to remove air bubbles.

Slide the flat washer on top of the fork spring before proceeding.

Tapping the fork leg gently on the work surface will allow the damper rod assembly to fall free.

Once cut to length, slide into the fork tube and tighten the damper rod screw at the bottom of the fork leg.

Reattach the top cap screw to the fork leg and tighten.

Place the second flat washer on top of the plastic spacer.

Slide the fork leg assembly into place and tighten the pinch bolt to secure.

After you have completed the first fork leg you can proceed to the second, repeating steps from page 45 through 49. Once the second leg is complete, and reinstalled, you can replace the front tire, axle and bolt. Be sure to retighten the axle pinch bolts to spec. Both brake calipers can also be bolted back in place and tightened. The upper triple tree can then be reinstalled, and secured with the steering stem nut and upper fork tube caps.

With the Star now lowered 1.5 inches in the front and 1 inch in the rear, you should notice an immediate change in the stance of the machine, and the alterations will become more apparent when you take to the open road. Be sure to check for proper lean angle when using the side stand on uneven pavement. The lower height of your Star will affect the way the bike rests on the stand, so be sure to allow adequate angle before walking away from a parked bike that has been lowered.

Reinstall the upper fork cover.

Chapter Three Part Number and Supplier

Page	Description	J&P Part #	Supplier name and part #
Pg. 35	Rear lowering kit	ZZ70407	Baron's BA-7520-00
Pg. 39	Progressive 420 series shock	ZZ70485	Progressive suspension 420-1040
Pg. 40	Baron's Lower Belt Guard	ZZ60073	Baron's BA-7428RD
Pg. 45	Baron's Front lowering kit	ZZ23160	Baron's BA-7522-00

Chapter Four

Setting Up Your Star for Touring

The Star Proves to be a Versatile Mount

Once you've upgraded the saddle and footboard accommodations, you will more than likely get an itch for longer days on the open road. To bring new levels of comfort and convenience to the equation we'll add a windshield, saddle-bags and some highway pegs. The highway pegs are combined with a tubular case guard, which can also make a great place to mount driving lights for added illumination after dark. All in all these additions will allow you to ride further in

You can see how Kody's boots ride high on the mounted foot pegs of the case guard giving you another riding position to break up a long day on the road.

greater comfort and that's what the riding world is all about.

There are a number of options when it comes to a fairing or windshield, so as with every other feature, shop around and see what fits your riding style the best. We have chosen a unit that can easily be removed while leaving the mounting hardware in place. This flexibility comes in handy when your riding changes from city to country, and back again, with any regularity.

Saddlebags are another arena that is full of players. Hard-sided, soft-side and almost everything in between can be had. Again, quick removal is key when changing your riding habits frequently. It's great to have a place to haul your needs on a road trip but cumbersome when simply tooling around town. The ability to remove the bags for security or convenience guided our choice, but your decision may be different.

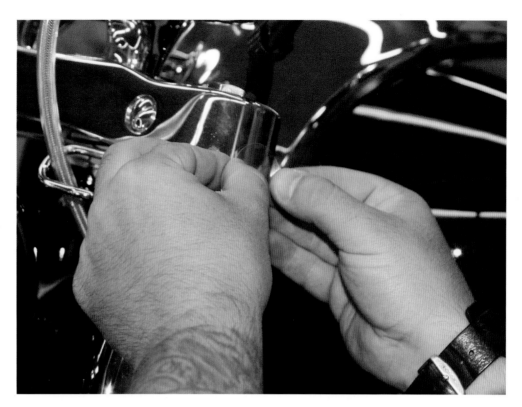

Maybe one of the best ways to add some comfort to your riding is a protective wind-shield. We will add the National Cycle Switchblade (J&P Part # ZZ75530) to the game. Begin by cleaning the surface, then applying the circular adhesive shields to the top of the fork legs.

The two-screw "spider" is held in place by a pair of metal bands that wrap around the fork tubes. Install the first band, then hang the "spider" as seen here.

Here we see the "spider" held in place by the upper and lower metal bands. These assemblies will be bound in place once the fairing mounts are attached.

Install the brass washer on the top threads before moving to the next step.

Once both sides of the fairing mounts are installed, line up the openings of the fairing with the hardware and press into place. The windshield will snap firmly and securely into position, but can be removed in minutes.

Before tightening the fasteners, make sure the "spider" is aligned with the fork tubes. Once straight, tighten each Allen head screw with a wrench.

As you can see in this illustration, the Switchblade windshield provides adequate protection while on the open road, but can be easily removed for riding around town.

To keep the bags from getting tangled in the wheels, we'll install a set of Cobra saddlebag supports (J&P Part # ZZ84054). Simply remove the screws holding the fender trim in place, then align the supports and reinstall using the supplied fasteners.

If you spend any time on the road you'll want a place to store some travel needs. A set of Saddlemen Midnight Express saddlebags (J&P Part # ZZ83242) will do the job nicely.

With the seat removed, and both supports installed, place the saddlebags over the top of the fender.

Insert the front seat bracket into the catch, then re-install the rear fastener to secure the saddle.

Get a leg up on the competition by adding a case guard and highway pegs. We have selected a Lindby Multibar (J&P Part # ZZ70970). Make sure you read the installation guide carefully

Remove the bolts that hold the floor-boards in place.

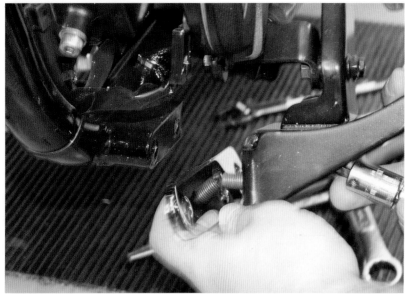

Place the lower support bracket between the frame and floorboard bracket and reinsert the factory fasten-er. DO NOT tighten now, only snug up the connection. Repeat the proce-dure on the other floorboard.

We'll need to drill two holes in the frame. Applying a piece of tape to the site will make it easier to see your drill marks.

Position the case guard and insert the two lower bolts, washers and nuts that secure it, but DO NOT tighten at this time.

With the lower bolts in place, the upper mounting bracket will now be in position. Mark the spot to be drilled with a marker. Drill an 11/32" hole through the steel and use the supplied bolt, nut and washer to secure. Tighten all fasteners once the guard in is position.

Chapter Four Part Number and Supplier

Page	Description	J&P Part #	Supplier name and part #
Pg. 51	National Cycle switchblade 2-up	ZZ75530	National Cycle N21107
Pg. 53	Saddlemen Midnight Express saddlebags	ZZ83242	Drag Specialties 3501-0058
Pg. 53	Cobra saddlebag supports	ZZ84504	Drag Specialties BLV26250
Pg. 53	Lindby Multibar	ZZ70970	Lindby Custom Inc. 13602

Chapter Five

Adding Trim to Personalize

Accents & Highlights

We are a country made up of people who enjoy being unique. While wearing your hair in a pink Mohawk is one way to show your personal style, many of us prefer to use our motorcycles. Riding a Yamaha is great but changing its appearance gives us a way to make it truly our own. There are a number of radical changes that can be made, but this chapter will address some of the simpler methods of dressing up your Star to meet your needs.

Once in place, the new chrome trim looks like an extension of the factory hardware.

With the shield removed you can see the entire section of the adhesive that will adhere to the motor.

One of today's terms for adding some chrome to your scoot is "bling". There's no way to determine who first coined the phrase, but I like it and will use it every chance I get. As with almost any project, you can add a little or a lot to the blend. Your taste and pocketbook are about the only factors that will dictate the level of trim you bring to the game.

The Yamaha we are building will end up with altered fenders and a custom paint job, but at this stage we are adding bling to the factory trim. This will be the starting point for most owners, so without wasting any more of your time, let's dig in.

Add bling with chrome push rod covers (J&P Part # ZZ97171) installed using double-sided adhesive, which is already attached to each piece. Once you have tested the fit of the piece, clean the surface.

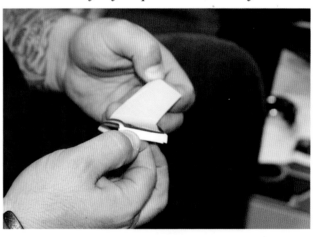

Peel the protective shield from the double-sided adhesive to expose the method of attaching to the motor. Be sure that the temperature of the room is not too hot or too cold to ensure proper adhesion of the new pieces.

Carefully locate the new trim on the motor before making contact. Once in place, push firmly to fix the chrome in position.

Moving down the push tubes, we will now install a tappet block cover set (J&P Part # ZZ97413). The area for the lower section is once again cleaned with the supplied alcohol swab before installation can occur.

The base of the tappet covers will be secured using the two blocks of double-sided adhesive. Remove the protective shields from each pad and press into position on the motor.

To secure each of the 2 lower push rod covers, remove the screw at the bottom of each tube.

With the chrome cover in place, reuse the factory screw to mount in place.

Now that we've added all three components of the tappet block covers, the motor has gotten another bit of bling.

To enhance breathing for our Road Star we are now adding a Baron's Big Air Cleaner kit. The Power Kone is first mounted to the chrome cover in the marked location using the double-sided tape that is on the Kone.

With the Power Kone attached, replace the back of the air cleaner assembly and use the Baron's screw to fasten the two pieces together.

Attach the three mounting brackets to the rear of the air cleaner in the locations molded into the piece.

Connect the Yamaha vent tube to the plastic fitting on the Baron's air cleaner and slide the spring clamp back into place to secure.

The Baron's Big Air unit mounts to the Yamaha locations and is held in place by three screws.

To finish off the lower end of each fork leg we are going to install a set of Baron's Bullet Fork Covers (J&P Part # ZZ22000).

Loosen, but DO NOT remove the retaining screw on each cover prior to installation.

Once the Baron's Big Air cleaner is in place, be sure to tighten the clamp at the rear of the unit that seals the carburetor to the airbox.

Test fit the piece before tightening the screw and check for adequate clearance for moving parts.

Once you are certain of the part's fit, tighten the retaining screw with an Allen wrench.

Although an easy add-on, the Bullet Covers bring a new level of "custom" to your Star.

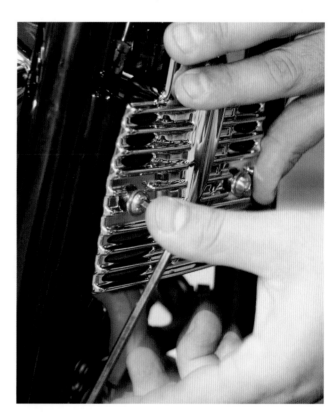

Next bit of bling is a chrome regulator cover from Kuryakyn (J&P Part # ZZ97175). It adds some flash to a typically overlooked component.

After removing the screws that hold the Yamaha part in place, position the chrome cover and use the supplied screws and washers to secure.

Nestled between the downtubes of the Yamaha frame the new cover brings some life to a dark corner of the Star.

Kuryakyn makes a set of Finned Spark Plug Covers (J&P Part # ZZ97416), and to install them you'll need to remove the seat and fuel tank for access.

To install the chrome cover on each cylinder you first need to remove the motor mount bolt.

Position the chrome part and check for fit before replacing the motor mount bolt.

Return the factory motor mount bolt to its original position and tighten to 35 foot-pounds.

Duplicate the actions for the second cylinder and you end up with a bit more bling on your Road Star.

The matte black section of the motor will now be adorned with a Kuryakyn Cylinder Base Cover (J&P Part # ZZ 97414) to bring some added flash to this side of the motor.

To gain access, you'll need to remove the shift linkage. Before doing so, mark the location of the linkage so the same splines can be used when returning the piece to its previous position.

Once you've marked the location of the linkage onto the shaft, loosen the screw that holds the parts together and slip the linkage off the splines.

Test fit the new cover to make sure you understand how it will be seated before moving ahead. A series of double stick pads will attach the piece to the motor, so wipe the area clean with the alcohol swab before placing the new part.

Once in place, the cover fills in another section of black with vivid chrome.

The second section of the cylinder base cover is held in place by using three screws already in place. Remove the three screws to install the new cover.

Each of the three removed screws will hold a new bracket in place. Follow the instructions carefully to ensure the proper location for each.

Position the new chrome cover over the three mounting brackets and double check for fit before inserting the mounting screws.

Use the supplied Allen head screws to fasten the cover in place.

Replace the shift linkage to the shaft and be sure to use your marks made earlier for proper alignment before tightening the retaining screw.

Chrome Boomerang Frame Trim (J&P Part # ZZ70414) will be next. On the right side, remove the two screws that hold the passenger footrest bracket in place.

Place the frame cover over the mounting holes, replace the passenger footrest, and reinsert the two screws to fasten to the frame.

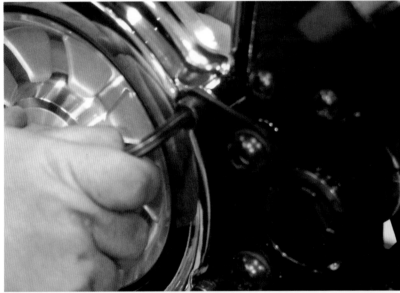

On the left side of the chassis you'll need to remove the two screws that hold the front pulley cover in place. The next two screws to be removed hold the passenger footrest in place.

Place the lower cover in position and use the two chrome screws supplied to secure.

The upper section of the left side cover can now be installed. Be sure to align the mounting holes of both brackets before replacing the passenger footrest.

Return the passenger footrest to its original location and secure with two fasteners.

With both sections of the left side frame covers in place you can see how they add some brightness to the previous black assembly.

A chrome swingarm cover set from Kuryakyn (J&P Part # ZZ97165) will now be used to dress up the tubes of that section of the chassis. Loosen and remove the rear axle adjusting nut.

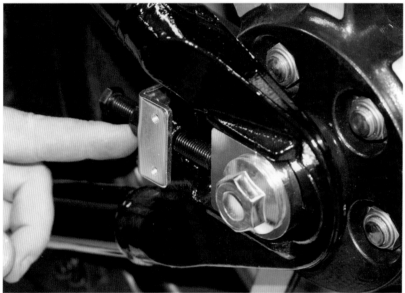

Slip the Kuryakyn receiver plate over the axle adjusting bolt and return the Yamaha nut to the end of the bolt.

To mount the cover you need to attach the inner bracket to the holes. Be sure that the bowed section of the bracket is facing out before inserting the screws. DO NOT tighten these two screws at this time.

Locate and test fit the upper cover before snapping into place. There are no screws used to secure the piece, only the curve of the cover to hold it in position.

Insert but DO NOT tighten the two screws at the front of the axle cover.

Snap the lower cover into place, and you now have two gleaming tubes instead of the glossy black members.

Use the Allen wrench supplied by Kuryakyn to tighten the two screws behind the cover, then you can fully tighten the two exposed screws from the previous step.

Place the chrome axle cover in position and make sure the mounting holes are lined up before inserting the screws.

With components on the left side now complete you can see the effect of the newly added chrome covers. The same basic steps are used to install the covers on the right side of the swingarm.

A Rear Master Cylinder Cover (J&P Part # ZZ97411) will further dress up the tail end of our Yamaha. Remove the screw that holds the factory cover in place to expose the master cylinder.

Wrap the lower section of the cover around the cylinder and secure with the original screw.

Clean the top of the cap with the alcohol swab to ensure adequate adhesion of the next piece.

Remove the protective film from the adhesive inside the chrome cover, then press into place over the existing master cylinder cap.

Same function with a new look, all in a few easy steps.

Chapter Five Part Number and Supplier

Page	Description	J&P Part #	Supplier name and part #
Pg. 57	Pushrod top covers	ZZ9717	Kuryakyn 7760
Pg. 58	Tappet block covers	ZZ97413	Kuryakyn 7728
Pg. 61	Baron's bullet fork covers	ZZ22000	Baron's BA-7800U
Pg. 62	Chrome regulator cover	ZZ97175	Kuryakyn 1544
Pg. 63	Finned spark plug covers	ZZ97416	Kuryakyn 7761
Pg. 64	Cylinder base cover	ZZ97414	Kuryakyn 7729
Pg. 67	Boomerang frame trim	ZZ70414	Kuryakyn 8662
Pg. 70	Swingarm cover set	ZZ97165	Kuryakyn 8262
Pg. 72	Rear master cylinder cover	ZZ97411	Kuryakyn 7825

Chapter Six

Lighting

Make it Cool, Make it Legal

By the time you've reached this chapter in the book you'll be no stranger to the idea that the Road Star can be modified in a number of ways to suit your needs. For some, the factory lighting will serve their needs just fine, but in our quest to build a hot rod Star we have decided to take a different path.

We will be eliminating much of the Yamaha lighting and trim, and replacing it with hardware that better fits the design of our project bike. The nice part of this is that you can choose to modify a single aspect of your Star, or work from a clean slate. A note of warning, when choosing to eliminate turn signals as we have here, make sure your

While retaining a mostly factory appearance we have boosted light output by installing the new headlamp.

state laws do not require illuminated turn indicators before you strip them off. It might look cool to ride around using hand signals when turning, but getting bluelighted takes the fun out of the game.

Choices in the headlight division are numerous, and our selection is based purely on aesthetics. Sure, the light we chose for installation has a different pattern than the stock bulb, but the fact that it looks great takes center stage. Changing the bulb in your factory headlamp is another way to enhance your ability to see after dark, but caution must be exercised to avoid the installation of a bulb that is simply too hot for use. There are some high wattage bulbs on the market that will literally melt wiring and the surrounding housing due to their extreme temperatures. A bright headlight is terrific, but a melted wire loom tends to dim the effect.

As in any alteration to wiring, or an electric circuit, care must also be taken to ensure that the new wiring is safely insulated and installed to avoid contact with bare metal. The application of heat shrink may seem excessive, but the time it takes is far less aggravating than trying to determine where the wires have shorted out in some hard to see location. Better safe than sorry.

Without getting your degree in electrical engineering, take some time to be sure the choices you make don't exceed the system requirements of your chosen machine. Amperage ratings must be closely adhered to in order to avoid a system meltdown or repeated fuse issues. A few moments of time up front will help you to reduce or eliminate electrical woes down the road.

With the rear fender back from the paint shop, we can now install the new tail light and license plate bracket.
Inset: To avoid troubles with rubbing the wires bare, we are inserting a rubber grommet into the hole where the taillight wires will pass through.

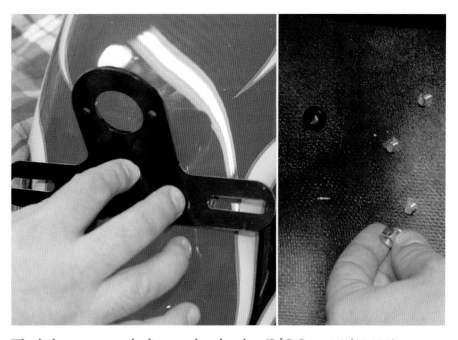

The holes to mount the license plate bracket (J&P Part # 3400120) were drilled prior to the custom paint so the bracket can quickly be put in place. Right: After inserting the three mounting screws through the drilled holes, fasten each with the nuts provided.

The Retro "Drilled" taillight (J&P Part # 340-390) will make a cool addition to our custom Star and is very bright despite its small size.

After attaching the license plate to the chrome frame (J&P Part # 970-986) you can attach it to the previously mounted bracket with the screws provided.

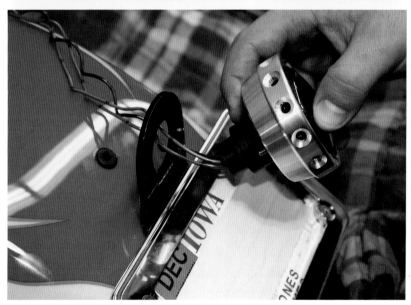

Pass the three wires of the taillight through the opening in the bracket, taking care not to scratch the new paint with the metal connectors.

Slide the back section of the taillight through the opening in the bracket, and hold in place until the two rear mounting screws have been tightened.

Using a screwdriver at the lens of the light allows you to tighten the screws at the back.

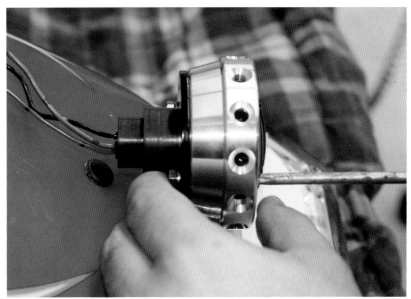

Carefully insert each of the three wires through the rubber grommet we installed in a previous step. The wires will be secured to the inside of the fender to avoid getting snagged on the rear tire.

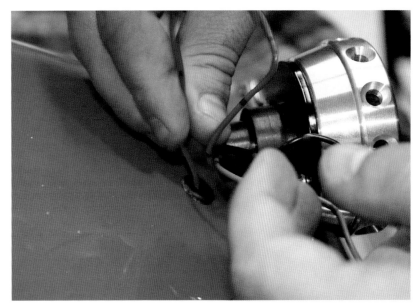

Our next alteration will be a headlight within the Yamaha housing. You can also opt to install an entirely new headlight assembly, but we'll simply upgrade the internals.

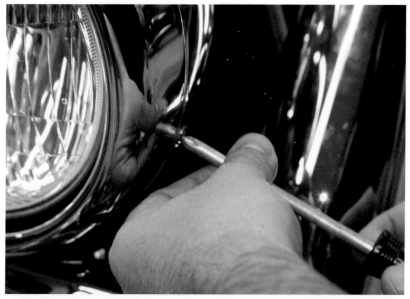

You will first need to remove the two screws that hold the trim ring in place and set them aside for reuse later.

Once the screws have been removed, you can remove the trim rind and headlight free of the bezel.

Carefully remove the plug that sends power to the bulb while keeping a solid grip on the headlight assembly.

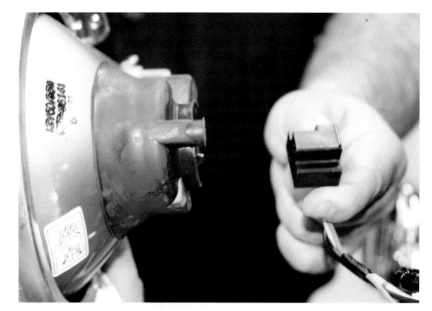

Arrange a soft cloth beneath the assembly before placing it on your work surface to avoid scratching the chrome trim ring.

Inset: Note the word "TOP" is molded into the rubber bulb cover, and the cover needs to be replaced in the same position when reassembling the headlight.

Lift the rubber bulb protector free of the assembly and set aside.

Unclip the wire bulb retainer and gently lift the bulb free of the headlight. WARNING! DO NOT touch the glass surface of the bulb with your fingers or skin. The oil from your skin will cause the bulb to burn out quickly.

We have chosen the Trillient 7" bulb from Adjure (J&P Part # 310-156) to replace the Yamaha lamp - for its high degree of style and improved light dispersion.

Here we can examine three styles of lamps that will easily fit the Yamaha assembly. The Adjure is on the left, the factory unit in the middle and a Delta Xenon unit is at the right. The cuts in the face of each lamp will create a different pattern, and make a big difference when riding at night.

With the bulb removed, unclip the wire retainer that holds the bulb assembly to the trim ring.

Before removing the two adjusting screws, make note of their position so they can be returned to the same setting upon reassembly.

The headlamp assembly can now be lifted free of the trim ring.

Remove the three screws that hold the headlamp to its mounting ring and again set them aside for reuse.

Place the new headlamp into the mounting ring.

When placing the new headlamp into the mounting ring be sure to align the tabs with the slots before reinstalling the three screws.

Having attached the headlamp to the mounting ring the assembly can now be set into the trim ring as before. Line up the new assembly with the adjustment screw locations.

Reinstall the two adjustment screws and their springs into the same position as they were before they were removed. Return the bulb into the opening in the rear of the headlamp, and replace the wire clip that holds it in place. Return the rubber bulb shield, making sure the "TOP" indication is located properly.

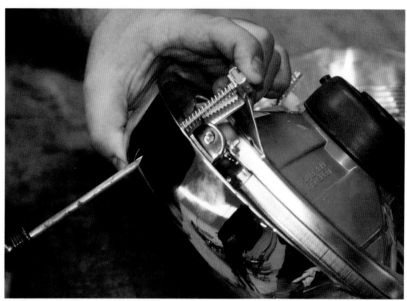

Here we see the new headlamp and bulb installed in the factory trim ring.

In keeping with our hot rod Star, we have selected to remove the front turn signal bar by pulling the two mounting screws - that are found just below the headlight bucket.

Unplug the wires that were connected to the turn signals and tuck them inside the headlight bucket for future use.

Reattach the three-pronged plug to the headlight assembly firmly making contact with the rubber bulb cover.

Line up the two mounting holes and place the revised headlight into the chrome bucket.

Inset: Replace the two screws that secure the trim ring to the bucket and tighten.

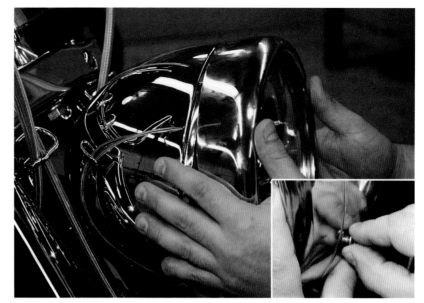

The new headlamp will give us a much better light pattern and look great while doing it.

Chapter Six Part Number and Supplier

Page	Description	J&P Part #	Supplier name and part #
Pg. 75	License backing plate	3400120	Custom Chrome 19885
Pg. 76	Retro "drilled" taillight	340-390	West Eagle 5348
Pg. 76	Billet License plate frame	970-986	J&P Cycles® exclusive
Pg. 80	Trillient 7" headlight bulb	310-156	Adjure T70300

Chapter Seven

Exhaust

Easy Bolt-On Power

Most of the chapters in this book are focused on altering the appearance, function or comfort of your Road Star. All of those factors will lead to a machine that is all you, but for many riders the first change will be the sound of their bike. The most efficient way of achieving this will be to exchange the factory exhaust with an aftermarket model. Before you go down that road, make sure you are comfortable with the fact that altering your Star in this way will VOID YOUR WARRANTY. A prudent path would be for a rider to spend some time on his or her new Star before

The factory pipes are nicely chromed and look terrific, but are a bit heavy and don't allow you to squeeze every drop of horsepower from the motor.

Loosen and remove the two bolts that hold the lower exhaust bracket in place.

Remove the floorboard to gain access to the existing hardware. Take time to ensure there are no space limitations when selecting a new exhaust system.

Each exhaust downtube connects to the motor with two bolts. Loosen and remove all four to begin the extraction of the Yamaha exhaust.

deciding what changes are needed. This would also allow your break-in maintenance to be done before making any radical alterations to your stock machine.

Yamaha and all other manufacturers of modern motorcycles spend millions of dollars to ensure that their offerings meet strict guidelines for noise levels and emissions. As rigid as the government is about enforcing these rules, there are none that keep a buyer from dropping the factory system in lieu of an alternate the moment he rides his motorcycle home. This train of thought doesn't make much sense, but it is what it is.

When you are ready to lift the exhaust system free of the bike, the small tang in the center of the rear bracket needs to clear the opening and will require an extra twist to remove.

To remove the exhaust, lift the muffler section with one hand.

Use a second hand to pull each exhaust downtube free of the motor, and the entire assembly can be lifted clear of the motorcycle.

The rear exhaust support now needs to be removed, so loosen and remove the two bolts that hold it to the frame.

Once you've decided to put on a new exhaust, there are many factors to consider. The most obvious will be the level of sound emitted from the new system. Each design lends itself to certain levels of noise and you need to check this out prior to running out to buy a new exhaust. For some, all they want is as much noise as possible. This "wisdom" usually doesn't take into account how the motor will function after bolting on some new tubes, but to some, noise is king. Most of us hope to add a bit of power to the machine, save some weight and maybe sacrifice on the whisper-quiet design that came with our new ride. For this breed of rider the world is your oyster and many options await you.

Another factor will be the appearance of your new system. A twin-cylinder motor limits some of these choices but still, options exist. Two-into-two, or a two-into-one design might suit your needs and tastes best. Some systems will work fine with the factory carburetor or fuel injection settings, but most will require a change there too. If you plan on adding a radically altered system like a shorty pipe with no baffles, you will more than likely need to re-jet the carburetor or adjust the mapping on your EFI. Before making any changes it's best to discuss the options with a certified mechanic or technician. Making the proper adjustments before taking to the streets will save you a lot of pain later. A poorly tuned setup will also make your altered machine run lean or rich, and will turn a set of clean chrome pipes a color you don't want, in a hurry.

When selecting a new pipe for your Star take note to find what will fit, how much more sound will be produced, and if it will operate with any added trim or accessories you've already bolted on. Following the manufacturers instructions carefully will also help you avoid leaks, as well as several other common maladies created by skipping steps or cutting corners. We have chosen three different sets of pipes and will show you how to install each one.

This steel loop is used to hold the rear brake line in place and is a part of the rear exhaust support. In order to remove the support you'll need to detach one end of the brake line.

Now removed from the chassis, we can see the rear exhaust support in its entirety.

Remove the banjo bolt on the rear caliper and keep it close because it will be reused in a moment.

The first set of pipes we'll install are Bub's Jug Huggers (J&P Part # ZZ47584). After opening the package, inspect the contents and review the instructions before starting.

The rear brake line retainer will also have to be removed before you can pull the exhaust bracket free.

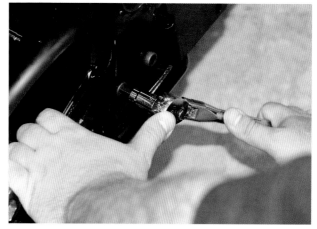

Position the Bub's exhaust bracket and use two Allen head screws and nuts. Use thread lock, but DO NOT tighten at this time.

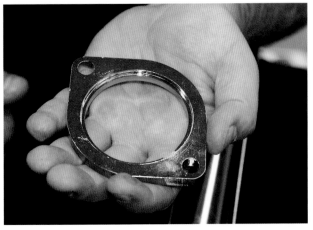

Per Bub's instructions, the exhaust flange will be installed with the grooved side towards the motor. The rear pipe will be the first to be added.

Slip the supplied bolt into the grooved channel on the back of the rear pipe.

Once the flange has been slipped over the end of the exhaust tube, use a supplied spiral clip to secure.

Place the rear exhaust section in position and insert, but DO NOT tighten the two fasteners at the motor. Use the washer and nut to secure the end of the pipe to the bracket, but DO NOT tighten yet.

Here is how the flange, spiral clip, and exhaust look prior to bolting it to the motor.

Place the second flange and spiral clip over the end of the front exhaust tube in the same way you did to the rear.

Position front exhaust tube and insert, but DO NOT tighten screws at the motor and bracket. Check for fit before tightening the four bolts at the motor to 14 foot/pounds. Tighten the bolts at the rear bracket.

Install the first exhaust flange over the exit end of the pipe and slide it up the length of the tube until it reaches the engine shoulder.

The next set of pipes come from Cobra. The HP series (J&P Part # ZZ49307) use a 2-into-1 design and have separate heat shields. Unpack box and inspect all components before beginning installation.

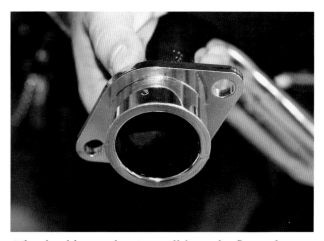

The shoulder on the pipe will keep the flange from going any farther, but can still rotate freely around the tube.

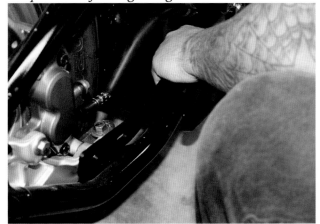

Install the Cobra lower support bracket using the supplied fasteners, but DO NOT tighten.

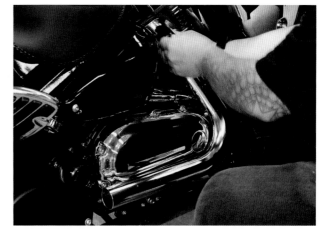

Install the first length of the system using the supplied hardware, but DO NOT tighten at this point.

After installing the exhaust flange over the second part of the exhaust, position it at the motor using the supplied hardware, but again, DO NOT tighten.

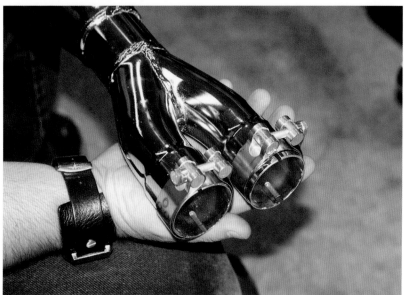

Slip the muffler clamps over the ends of the assembly. By positioning the bolts in opposite directions (one up and one down) you will be able to easily tighten them once the rest of the components are in place.

With the clamps in place, slide the muffler over the ends of the two sections of exhaust already in place.

Secure the muffler to the lower support bracket using the two Cobra bolts, but as before, DO NOT tighten yet.

Tighten each of the muffler clamps when you are satisfied that the rest of the parts are aligned properly, and adequate clearance is determined.

Test fit each section of heat shield before proceeding. There are three pieces for the shield so be sure you understand how they go together before starting.

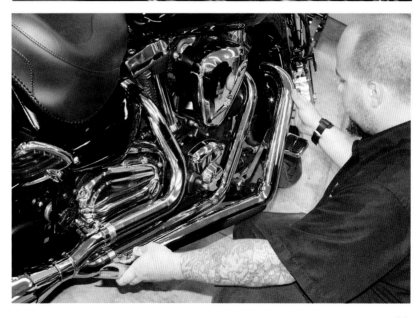

Each section of the heat shield is held in place by adjustable hose clamps. Slide a hose clamp into the slots inside the shields, but leave them open. Once the clamps are attached, slide each section of heat shield into place and tighten them snugly. The remaining hardware can now be tightened to factory specs.

Now installed, we can see how the Cobra two-into-one design allows more room for saddlebags, and will also boost power while saving a few pounds of weight.

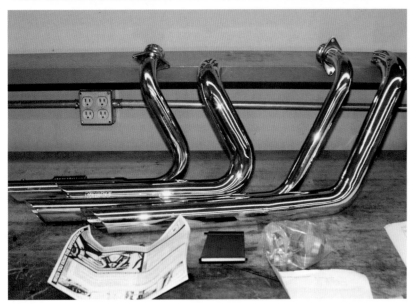

Our final set of pipes are from Vance & Hines. The Shortshot Staggered (J&P Part # ZZ49037) are a two-into-two configuration, and also have separate heat shields.

The Vance & Hines mounting bracket will attach to the chassis with the supplied bolts and nuts.

A small amount of thread lock should be used on each bracket mounting bolt to hold it securely.

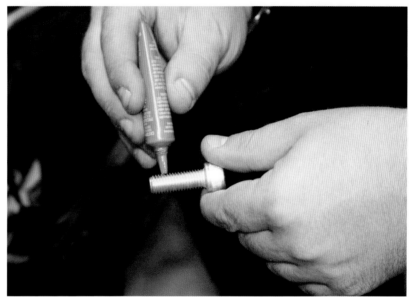

Following Vance & Hines' directionss, carefully mark the location of the heat shield clamps on the edge of the shield so it can be seen once they have been assembled.

Slip the exhaust pipe through the clamps to attach the heat shields.

To avoid scratching the chrome on the exhaust pipes, keep the clamps in an open position until the pieces are completely in place.

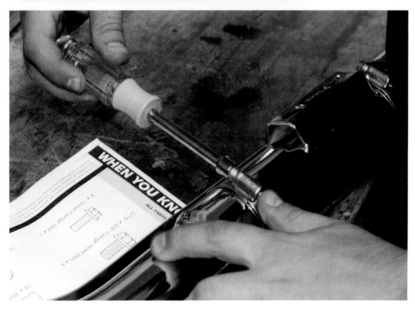

Once the heat shield is in place you can tighten the screws of the clamps to secure.

Slide the supplied receiver plate into the slotted channel on the back of the exhaust so you can mount the system to the support bracket later.

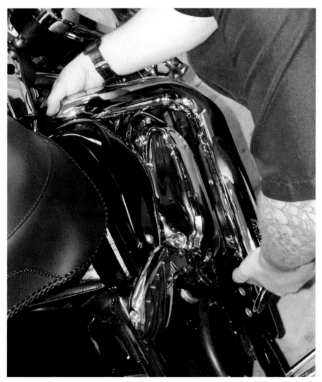

Position the rear pipe and install the two upper bolts before inserting the lower fasteners. DO NOT tighten yet.

Place the front section of the exhaust in its mounting location and fasten the upper bolts before adding the lower ones.

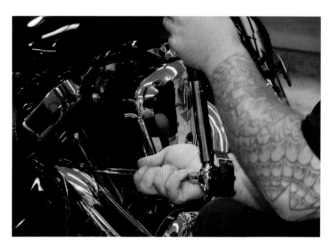

Once you are satisfied with the fit and clearance, you can tighten the upper bolts to 14 foot/pounds each.

The Vance & Hines pipes will really bring some fresh bark to the Road Star and their design will blend perfectly with the rest of the theme.

Before you can reinstall the floorboard you'll need to add the spacer provided by Vance & Hines. Remove the Yamaha mount to continue.

After using thread lock on the bolt, place the spacer between the chassis and the bracket to provide the needed gap between the board and the pipes.

Once the bracket and spacer have been tightened you can return the floor board to its original mounting holes with the factory hardware.

With the Vance & Hines system installed and the floorboards back in their place we are ready for a test ride.

Chapter Seven Part Number and Supplier			
Page	**Description**	**J&P Part #**	**Supplier name and part #**
Pg. 89	Bub Jug Huggers	ZZ47584	BUB Enterprises 14-1202CG
Pg. 91	Cobra HP Series	ZZ49307	Drag Specialties 1810-0538
Pg. 94	Vance and Hines Short Shot Staggered	ZZ49037	Drag Specialties 1810-0558

Chapter Eight

Carburetor, Manifold, Air Cleaner

More Air Equals More Power

Now that you've replaced the factory exhaust with a better breathing system, the carburetion and other intake components need to be addressed. By improving the efficiency of the exhaust, the parts of the motor that draw breath also need to be upgraded to ensure proper performance at all levels.

Just as replacing the exhaust will more than likely void your warranty, some of the changes listed in this chapter are also against the manufacturer's rules. When Yamaha designs and builds their motorcycles they must adhere to a strict set of

Plug in the wire loom on the back of the dash panel and reinstall using the three factory screws.

To provide easier access to the components in question, we will remove the fuel tank first. Loosen the three fasteners that hold the dash in place.

the openings of the molded manifold you can see how the interior corners have been beveled to permit a smoother airflow, thus improving performance.

Before starting any work on your Yamaha, read the instructions from the part supplier carefully. This small step will help you avoid some costly errors as the project begins, and make the entire job more pleasant. It is far better to be well prepared, versus wading into the deep end of the pool before checking how well you can swim.

guidelines to meet with federal limits. Standards on noise, emissions and efficiency all must be followed to the letter in order to sell motorcycles. When staying within these parameters, certain aspects of your Road Star's performance will be affected. I'm sure that Yamaha would love to build a no-holds-barred machine to dominate the market, but "big brother" frowns on that sort of fun.

Some of the revisions to the carburetor are also fairly delicate and not something that can be handled by an inexperienced owner. None of these steps are akin to brain surgery, but still require a deft hand.

We'll be installing a set of components produced by Baron's and every part of the kit has been designed to work together. Omitting any of the items will sacrifice performance and therefore cancel your efforts even before you start the motor. The Smooth Big Air Carb Kit comes complete with everything you'll need to improve the function of your carburetor and air cleaner. This is very important after installing an exhaust that allows spent fumes to flow more freely. We have also chosen to install the Baron's Ported Manifold to further enhance breathing. When you look into

Once free, unplug the wire loom that is hidden beneath and set aside the panel.

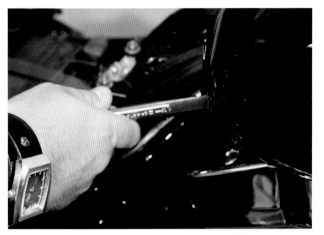

Loosen the bolt from the rear of the fuel tank to begin its removal.

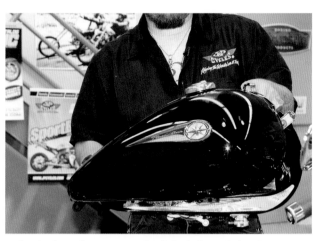

The fuel tank can now be lifted free of the frame, exposing the hardware we now need to address.

Lift the tank slightly and unplug the harness between the frame and the tank. Pull the breather hose from the tube at the front of the tank.

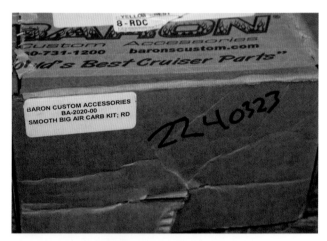

Baron's Smooth Big Air Carb Kit (J&P Part# ZZ 40323) comes complete with everything you'll need to revise your Road Star's intake of oxygen.

Switch the fuel valve to "off", then place an absorbent cloth beneath the fuel petcock before pulling the rubber fuel line off of the nipple.

Loosen the three Allen-head bolts that hold the Yamaha air cleaner assembly in place.

Use a screwdriver to loosen the clamp that holds the air cleaner to the mouth of the carburetor.

The factory air cleaner can now be pulled free of the carburetor. Once removed, you can pull off the two rubber hoses that are attached to the rear of the air cleaner assembly.

Use an Allen wrench to loosen the clamp holding the carburetor to the manifold.

A 10mm wrench is used to loosen the nuts that hold the throttle cables in place. Once the cables are free their ends can be pulled from the plate on the carburetor.

The carb can now be pulled off. CAUTION! There are still a few wires, and a rubber hose, that need to be removed before the carb will be free of the motor!

You can now see the remaining lines that need to be pulled before taking the next steps.

Loosen the nut that holds the choke cable in place and free it from its mounting point.

Use an absorbent cloth to catch any fuel before you pull the line from the fuel pump. The carb heater line, throttle position sensor, and idle speed adjust cable also must be loosened moorings before the carb will be free.

This illustration shows the connectors and lines that need to be disconnected before the carb can be taken to the bench for the next steps.

Place the carburetor upside-down on the work bench and remove the 4 screws that hold the float bowl in place. The factory screws are prone to stripping and will be replaced by Baron's parts when reassembling.

Loosen the nut that holds the carb heater in place and twist the bracket to the side.

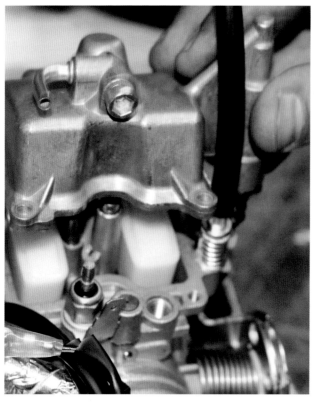

Carefully lift the float bowl off of the carburetor body. A small amount of fuel may be left in the bowl so be sure to capture any spillage before moving on.

With the bowl removed you get a clear view of the main jet that will be replaced.

Remove the factory main jet from the carb by loosening with a screwdriver, then unscrewing the last few threads by hand.

Thread the Baron's replacement main jet into place by hand first, then tighten with a screwdriver.

Replace the float bowl cover.

Using the 4 Allen head screws provided, attach the bowl to the carb and tighten equally. CAUTION!!! Excess force is NOT required to secure these screws in place.

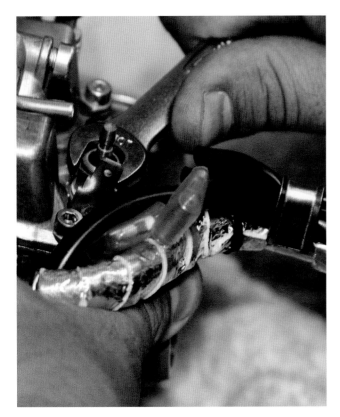

Twist the carb heater bracket back into place and tighten the nut to secure in place.

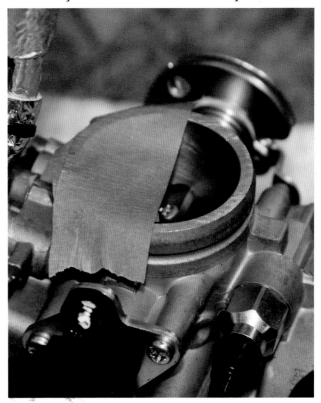

To keep debris from entering the carburetor, tape the mouth closed.

This next step will make your Road Star run much better, but WILL void any warranty left from Yamaha. Use the bit provided and drill out the idle air screw plug. Use caution to avoid going deeper than required.

With the plug now drilled and removed, you can see the idle air adjustment screw that lies beneath.

Using a flat-bladed screwdriver, turn the air adjustment screw all the way IN. Now carefully turn the screw OUT 3 rotations.

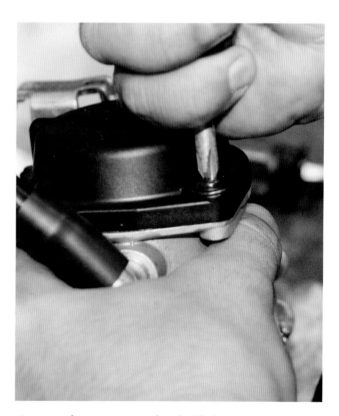

Remove the two screws that hold the constant velocity (CV) cover in place. CAUTION! Parts beneath this cover are small and include coil springs. Take extra care not to lose any of these small parts.

With the cover removed you can see the delicate spring that lies beneath.

Carefully remove the thin rubber vacuum slide and the spring. The vacuum slide is delicate and needs to be kept clean and free of damage to function properly.

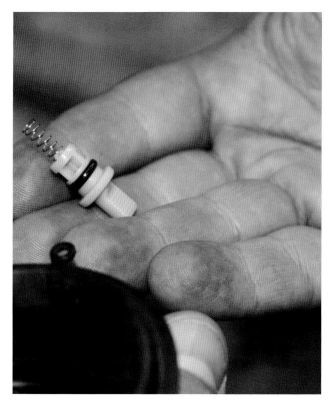

This assembly is the next to be removed, and will be reused as it is, so keep it handy and free of debris.

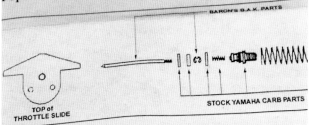

um slide from the carburetor.

l needle, spacer and washers, noting order of assemb

top to the bottom, install the new **Baron needle**
needle. The top is the blunt end of the needle.

l spacer and washers as shown in the figure below.

BARON'S B.A.K. PARTS

TOP of
THROTTLE SLIDE

STOCK YAMAHA CARB PARTS

um slide along with the diaphragm spring.

ragm cover back and tighten its screws.

Note: *Verify that the slide maintains its fu*

the float bowl and remove the bowl cover.

nlace it with a Baron's genuin

The Baron's instruction sheet illustrates which parts will be used again, and which are included in the kit.

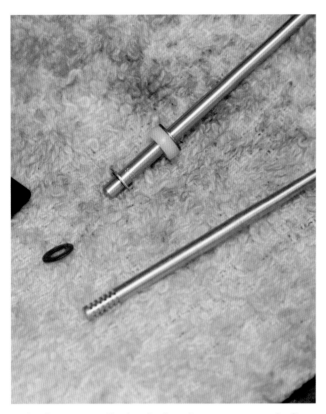

The factory needle (with the plastic ring attached) is not as tapered as the Baron's replacement unit and therefore does not allow as much fuel.

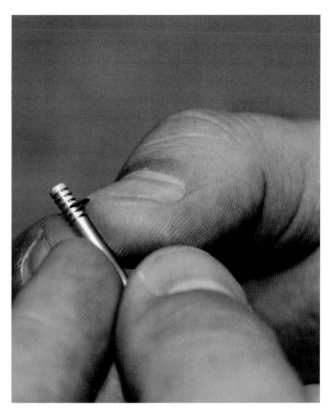

Use the "C" clip from the factory needle and place on the fourth groove, as instructed by the Baron's directions.

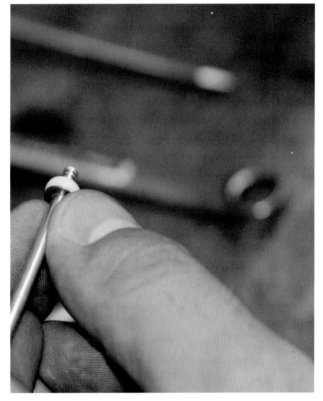

Place the factory plastic collar on top of the "C" clip.

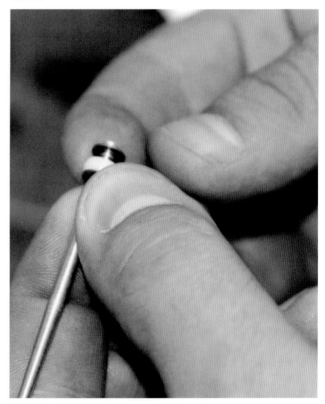

Place the factory washer over the end of the needle and against the white plastic collar.

Slide the Baron's needle assembly back into the vacuum slide with the tapered end down.

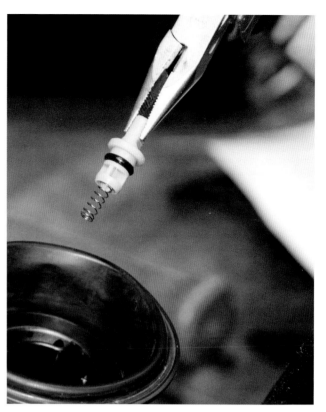

Replace the plastic spring assembly back over the needle within the vacuum slide.

Slip the vacuum slide components back into the body of the carburetor.

Be sure that the vacuum slide is placed with this loop settled into the matching notch for a proper seal when reassembled.

Replace the CV cover and reattach with the 2 factory screws. We're replacing the Yamaha manifold with the Baron's Ported Manifold (J&P Part# ZZ 40596).

Slowly pull the fuel pump assembly free of the bracket.

To gain access to the factory manifold you must first loosen the two bolts that secure the fuel pump to the frame bracket.

Remove the two Allen head bolts that secure the manifold to the cylinders of the motor.

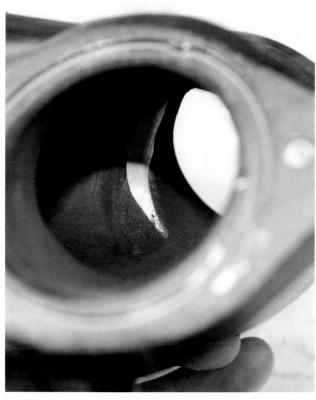

The bright spots inside the Baron's Ported Manifold are where sharp corners have been beveled, allowing for smoother airflow through the piece.

Pull the Yamaha manifold from between the cylinders.

Remove the "O" rings from the Yamaha manifold and slip them in place on the Baron's unit.

The new manifold fits in the same place as the factory model and requires no fiddling for a proper fit.

Bolt the new manifold in place using the factory hardware, tightening to factory torque specifications.

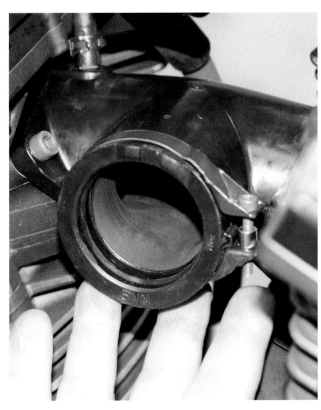

Place the Yamaha carburetor clamp back over the mouth of the Baron's manifold, but do not tighten.

Reconnect all lines, hoses, and wire looms before slipping the re-jetted carb back into place and tightening the clamp on the mouth of the manifold.

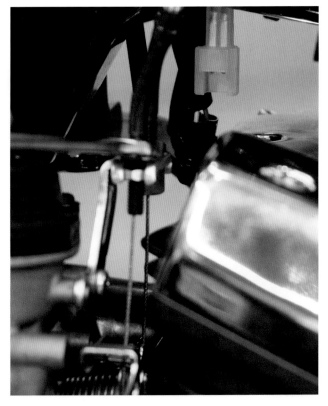

Reattach the throttle cables into the plate, then tighten nuts to secure in place. Check for smooth motion before proceeding.

114

Slide the idle adjustment control back into place by securing the grooved white collar into the brass colored slot seen here.

Expose the adhesive on the face of the Baron's Power Kone and affix to the backside of the new air cleaner faceplate by using the inscribed lines.

Place the air cleaner element and back plate in position, and use the Baron's hardware to secure to the chrome faceplate.

Again using the Baron's hardware, attach the three mounting brackets to the back plate of the air cleaner assembly.

Before mounting the new air cleaner in place be sure to reattach the rubber vent hose to the rear of the assembly.

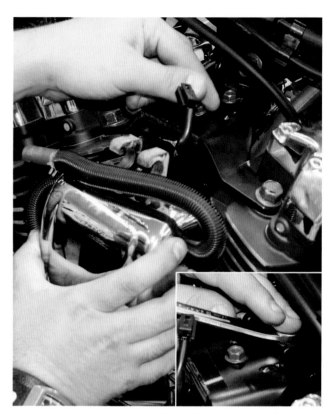

The fuel pump assembly can be reinstalled using the same 2 10mm bolts and factory bracket. Inset: Line up holes in bracket and pump, install bolts and tighten.

The air cleaner assembly mounts to the same three points as the factory unit, replace the screws to secure. Tighten clamp that holds air cleaner to the carb.

Reattach the lines and connectors, and slip them into their support clamps.

The new Baron's Smooth Big Air Carb Kit looks great on the Road Star and will enhance performance as well.

Place the choke cable back into its factory bracket and tighten the securing nut.

Slide the fuel tank back into position, and reconnect all wire looms and hoses before bolting in place.

Chapter Eight Part Number and Supplier

Page	Description	J&P Part #	Supplier name and part #
Pg. 102	Baron's smooth Big Air Kit	ZZ40323	Baron's BA-2020-08
Pg. 112	Baron's ported Manifold	ZZ40596	Baron's BA-5524-01

Chapter Nine

Wheels Go Round and Round

Wheels Define a Custom Bike

One of the most dramatic changes you can make to your Star is the installation of aftermarket wheels and tires. This alteration will usually save you some weight, and a lighter machine rides and handles better, as well as adding some value to the purchase.

Once the decision has been made to bolt-on a new set of rims, care must be taken for proper fitment and installation. There are many makers of custom rims for motorcycles, so take your time and find the style that best suits your needs and tastes. Once a design has been selected you

A set of chrome wheels from Performance Machine called "The Gasser". J&P offers more than 20 styles of wheels to fit your Star, so check with them for the latest designs.

also need to be sure wheels for your specific make and model are available. While all wheels are round and hold a tire in place, their applications are very specific. Wheel width, diameter and hub configuration all play into the theme, and must be followed to the letter.

As desirable as adding a huge rear donut may be, the factory swingarm will dictate what can and can't be used. Once again, doing your homework and ordering the wheels that fit your design and mechanical needs will always bring a happy ending to the project. Any deviation in the tire's diameter will affect your speedometer and tach, giving you erroneous information. The profile of your chosen tires must also fall within the limits set by Yamaha to deliver safe cornering. Both front and rear tires should share a similar profile; or your new rubber will cause your Star to tip into corners, or be resistant to turn at all. The compound of your tires must also be considered - and chosen based on your style of riding. Racing tires are the stickiest around, but their lifespan is far shorter than most riders care to deal with on a street legal machine. The weight of the rider, passenger, and possible luggage must also be considered when buying fresh skins. Your local dealer or online supplier can

A solo saddle adds comfort for the rider, but leaves a passenger standing on the curb. The added chrome trim spices up the swingarm and brings it to the same level as the rest of the machine.

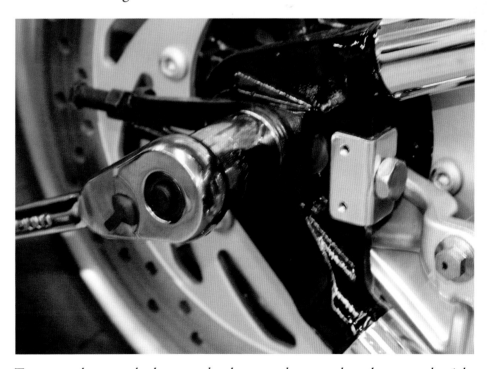

To remove the rear wheel you need to loosen and remove the axle nut on the right side of the chassis. The bike should be raised with a jack to lessen the weight in the rear wheel for easier removal.

119

Once the nut has been loosened you can remove the nut, washer, and belt adjuster, allowing the axle to be pushed through the wheel assembly.

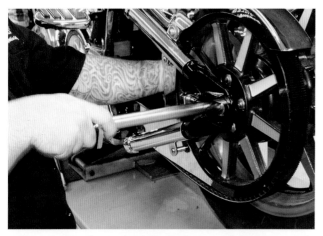

The axle can be pushed through from the right, while being pulled free on the left.

Slide the wheel forward enough to gain some free play in the belt. Slip the belt from the drive pulley to allow removal of the tire and wheel.

guide you to the proper rubber that will suit your riding and budget.

Once the new hoops have been chosen many riders opt to also change the brakes and drive pulleys to match the new wheels. Once again, searching for these items can be a rewarding process, but even more care must be taken to ensure correct fit and function. For this build we selected a set of Performance Machine wheels named "The Gasser". We selected an 18" rim to replace the factory 16" so our instruments will give us a false reading at all speeds. The overall difference in size isn't drastic, but enough to throw things off. Since this bike will probably never see any action, the look was more important than the accuracy of the gauges.

For illustration purposes we will also be adding Performance Machine rotors and calipers to complete the package. When swapping out the parts as a set you get a much more coherent appearance, but the cost gets a bit high for some. To alleviate the expense, Performance Machine also sells adapters that allow you to use your original Yamaha rotors with Performance calipers, saving some dough. You can always step up and add new rotors at a later date to complete your own project on a step-by-step basis.

Before beginning a change of this magnitude, be sure to carefully read all instructions and factory guidelines for the components being used. Abiding by "Read three times, install once," will save you countless hours of work, versus trying to make things work your way.

Hundreds of hours of R&D have gone into the creation of your after market parts, and the chosen manufacturer wants your installation process to go as painlessly as possible.

The new look your scooter will achieve by using custom rims will be amazing, and following the instructions to the letter will ensure they work as great as they look.

With the axle removed and the belt pulled from the pulley, the rear wheel can be slipped free of its location.

Using a 7/32" Allen wrench, you need to remove the five bolts that hold the adapter plate to the wheel.

Here is the standard Yamaha wheel compared to the new PM wheel, and Avon tire. The new combination is slightly taller, but the tire has a lower profile for a more aggressive appearance and improved handling.

With the five bolts removed you can pull the adapter plate free of the wheel. It will not be needed now, but can be saved for use if you return your bike to stock.

New Gatlin SS rotors from PM add flash and match the wheels. Contact your J&P technician to see what styles of rotors are available to compliment your chosen wheels.

Prior to installing the new pulley, you need to place the pulley adapter hub onto the wheel.

Place the pulley on the wheel once the hub adapter has been installed.

The adapter plates also need to be removed from the front wheel before you can mount the new brake discs.

The inner hub spacer must now be put in place prior to bolting the pulley to the wheel.

Use the five bolts and thread lock provided by Performance Machine to attach a brake rotor to each side of the front wheel.

Use the bolts, and thread lock, supplied by PM to attach the pulley to the wheel. Tighten each of the bolts to 55 foot/pounds. Repeat these steps to mount the brake disc to the opposite side of the rear wheel.

Install and hand tighten each of the fasteners to ensure proper fit before tightening in place.

Tighten each of the bolts to 55 foot/pounds per the Performance Machine specs. These steps will be repeated to attach the second disc to the wheel.

Lift the new wheel and tire into position and slip the drive belt back onto the new pulley.

Loosen and remove the banjo bolt from the Yamaha caliper on the right side of the wheel. Keep a cloth handy to catch any leaking brake fluid before it touches any finished surfaces.

Place the Performance Machine wheel spacer on the left side of the wheel before sliding the axle back into position.

Loosen and remove the bolt that holds the rear caliper to the frame.

The rear axle can now be slid back into place, but DO NOT pass it completely through the wheel assembly until the next step is complete.

A second spacer and the rear caliper bracket, provided by Performance Machine, must be installed on the right side of the wheel before the axle can be passed through and secured.

For fasteners, PM supplies high quality chrome Allen bolts.

The Performance Machine caliper is secured to the bracket using the two fasteners provided. DO NOT tighten the fasteners until the remaining assembly has been installed.

Install the first end of the Performance Machine anchor rod to the chassis, as illustrated in the instructions.

Again using the hardware provided, mount the second end of the anchor rod to the caliper mounting bracket.

The new location of the brake caliper will require the use of an extended brake line for proper operation. Your J&P technician can guide you through this process to ensure the correct length and fittings. Once the brake line has been installed you need to bleed the line. This can be done now, or after the front brakes have been installed.

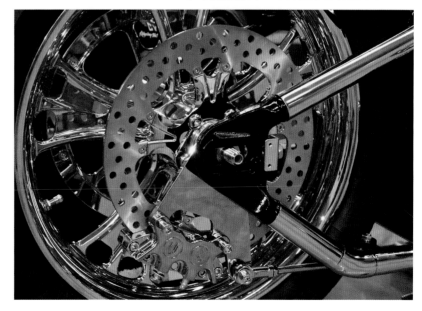

Loosen, but DO NOT remove the banjo bolt on each of the front brake calipers, and at the upper junction box between the fork legs. Be sure to use a cloth to catch the fluid as it drips from the loosened fittings. Remove the bolts that secure the caliper to the right fork leg.

Remove the bolt that holds the left caliper in place, and pull both calipers free of the rotors.

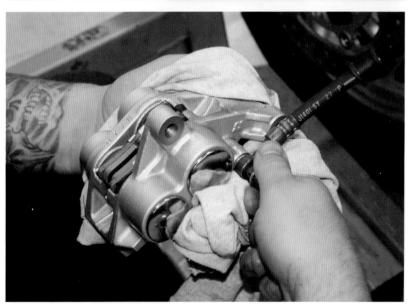

Place a cloth beneath each rotor before removing the banjo bolt completely.

Remove the upper banjo bolt and pull the factory brake line assembly free of the front end.

Remove the pinch bolt at the bottom of the right fork leg, then loosen the front axle.

Performance Machine provides you with a selection of shims to provide the proper spacing between the rotor and brake pads.

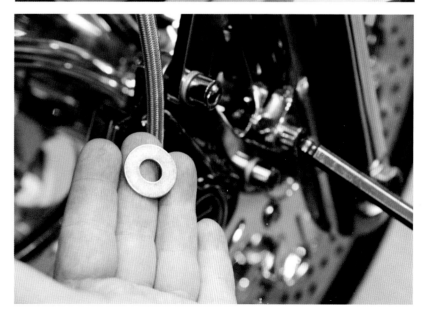

The use of the custom handlebars will require the installation of extended brake lines for the front calipers. Once again your J&P technician can guide you through the process to ensure you order the proper length. Attach the end of each line to the front calipers and tighten to specifications.

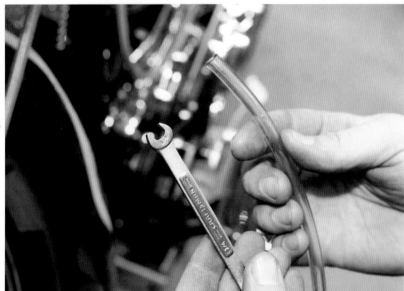

Once all the fittings for the brake lines have been tightened, you need to bleed the excess air from the lines. A small wrench and length of plastic tubing are the simple tools required. If you are not comfortable with the process we suggest, you can have an experienced technician do the job.

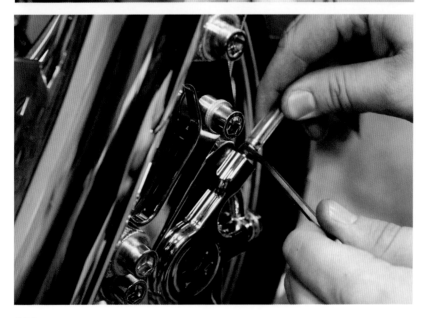

Place the plastic tubing over the fitting, and pump the brake lever and hold before you loosen the connection enough to allow the brake fluid to flow into the tube.

Squeezing the brake lever will force the fluid through the system and into the tube. Once the fluid stops flowing you can tighten up the bleeder. These steps must be done while maintaining pressure on the lever at the grip. (If you release the lever while the bleeder is still open air will be drawn back up into the caliper). Repeat this process until all air bubbles have been purged from the line.

The sky high bars add some new attitude to the Star, and our aftermarket headlight will shine new light on the road after dark. Right: This view is what most other riders see as our altered Yamaha rolls away from them at every opportunity. The bobbed rear fender and retro taillight show the crows how its done.

Chapter Ten

Changing Fenders and Fuel Tank

Make it a Real Custom Machine

One of the most dramatic ways to change the look of your Road Star is to alter the appearance of the fenders and fuel tank. To achieve this you can go about it in several ways. The first method involves modifying the sheet metal that comes on your bike to take on new dimensions or contours.

Not all of us have access to the proper sheet metal tools required to take this route, but for those that do, a world of alterations can be made.

The route we will follow involves removing the stock fenders and replacing them with more stylish fiberglass units. We will show you the way

With our new fenders in place we can stand back and view the results of the altered body work and custom paint.

to install the new fenders in their unpainted form. This permits you to view the new fenders in position so you can determine if additional changes will need to be made before the new paint goes on. The factory fuel tank will also be removed, but only to receive a custom paint job before being reinstalled. There is a long list of options that can be employed to change the contours of the fuel tank, but in keeping with the "hot rod" nature of this build, the proportions of the Yamaha tank will work great.

If you aren't in the mood to completely revise the fenders on your own Star, there are a number of add-ons that can be used to dress up the Yamaha bits. Chrome trim, lighting, and a variety of bolt-on accessories can be used to spiff up your cruiser to suit your personal tastes.

As we have already mentioned time and time again, be sure to check for proper fit with any changes you make to your Yamaha. New components bring new dimensions to the equation, and safe operation is still a key, no matter how cool you want to look. Correct suspension travel, clearance of cables and wires, as well as handlebar motion must all be considered when altering the factory hardware. Yamaha spends countless hours to ensure the bike you buy is safe so alterations must be made carefully to maintain the same level of pain free riding. A great looking custom bike is one thing, but a full body plaster cast is another.

A pair of fiberglass Bob'd fenders from Baron's (J&P Part # ZZ71290, front and ZZ71961 rear) will make the transition from stock to hot rod a breeze. Custom paint will later be added to really bring some new life to the Road Star.

Remove the seat before changing the fenders using the ignition key, and unbolting the rear fastener. Loosen and the nut on the top mounting bolt, but leave the bolt in place for now.

Remove the two bolts at the lower edge of the rear fender.

Prior to installing the Baron's fender, make sure the hardware fits properly. Once the hardware has been checked, the new fender can be put in place and the Yamaha bolt can be reinstalled.

Unplug the connectors for the taillight wiring.

With the new fender now in place, we can see how much different it appears when compared to the factory piece. The custom paint will add some real excitement.

While holding the rear fender in one hand, remove the long bolt from the top mounting position and lift the fender free of the chassis.

A pair of 3/8-16x1" bolts, nuts and washers will be used to hold the lower edge of the fender in place. Reattach the nut to the top mounting bolt to complete the rear fender installation.

Each side of the front fender is held in place by two bolts. Remove the two from one side of the fork and set aside.

When you remove the rear mounting bolt, it will free the reflector mount. Move the reflector aside to expose the two holes of the fender mounts.

Repeat the removal of the two bolts on the left side of the fork to remove the fender.

With all four bolts removed you can lift the fender from the fork legs. As with the rear fender, set the factory parts in a safe place in case you decide to return the bike to stock later on.

The mounting tabs will need to be drilled for the new front fender before you can install it.

To remove the two fork reflectors you need to loosen the banjo bolts on the brake line before slipping them off. Be sure to use a cloth to catch any brake fluid to keep it from coming in contact with other surfaces.

Hold the new fender in place to check were the holes will need to be drilled. This allows you to check for proper clearance of the tire and related mounting hardware before you drill.

To ensure the proper location of the new fender mounting holes, place a piece of tape over the factory fender mounts and cut them out with a razor knife.

Pull the cut tape from the Yamaha fender and place in on the new Baron's unit in the location determined a few steps back.

With the tape applied to the new fender, put it back in place to be sure the holes will line up with the fork mounting locations one final time before drilling.

Using a block of wood to support the new fender, center punch each location to be drilled.

After completing the center punching of all four holes, remove the tape from the fender.

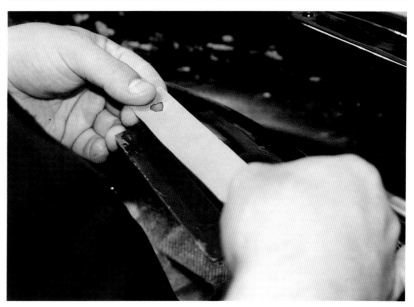

First drill each of the punch marks with a small pilot drill bit.

Using the pilot holes to guide you, select a 11/32" drill bit to open up each hole to the proper diameter.

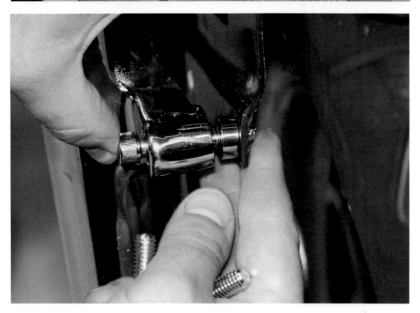

When reinstalling your new fender, you'll need to use a spacer, as shown, at each mounting point for proper spacing.

After loosely installing the hardware on one side of the fender, you can repeat the process on the other fork leg.

With the new front fender mounted we can see how much trimmer it is than the Yamaha one it replaced. The next section will cover the installation of the freshly painted fenders and fuel tank. Take extra caution not to scratch the new paint when inserting bolts and fasteners.

Since we already installed the new taillight in Chapter 6, the painted fender can be moved into place for installation.

Align the upper mounting hole in the fender with those on the frame, and insert the Yamaha bolt through until the threads are exposed on the opposite end.

Replace the Yamaha nut onto the end of the bolt and tighten to specifications.

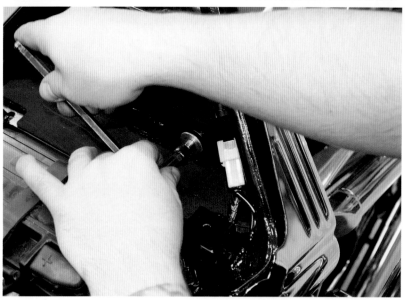

Use the same two fasteners as before to secure the lower edge of the fender to the frame, and tighten securely. Reconnect the taillight wires before continuing.

With the fuel tank just back from the painters, you'll need to remove the masking and excess paint from the vent tube fitting before attaching the line.

Inset: Reattach the factory mounting brackets to the underside of the fuel tank in the same position they were before disassembly.

Kody carefully lowers the painted fuel tank into position and seats it on the rubber tank pads on the frame.

When properly seated, the tank will rest in a position that allows for adequate clearance for the lines and wires that run underneath.

Reattach the connectors to the underside of the instrument panel, making sure they are returned to the proper mate.

The instrument panel can now be lowered into place, again taking care to position the wires where they won't get pinched when things are tightened in place.

Confident the wiring beneath is in place, the instrument panel can be set into its mounting position.

Gently adjust the position of the panel to align the mounting hole in the tank, with the one in the chrome trim.

Our chosen saddle will mount into the slot seen near the upper fender mounting bolt, and use the Yamaha retainer clasp to hold it in place.

Return the Yamaha fastener to its original position, and tighten to secure the instrument panel to the tank.

First insert the rear mounting tab of the Saddlemen Renegade Solo seat (J&P Part # ZZ80768) into the slot at the rear, then snap the front bracket into the retainer clasp.

Chapter Ten Part Number and Supplier

Page	Description	J&P Part #	Supplier name and part #
Pg. 131	Baron's bob'd fenders Front	ZZ71290	Baron's BA-9120-01
	Baron's bob'd fenders Rear	ZZ71961	Baron's BA-9220-01
Pg. 141	Saddlemen Renegade Solo seat	ZZ80768	Drag Specialties Y3370J

inspiration!

Your imagination is your only limitation. Let J&P Cycles® supply you with all the parts and technical know-how you need to make your wildest dreams a reality.